ACCOMPLICE TO EVIL

Also by Michael A. Ledeen

The Iranian Time Bomb
War Against the Terror Masters
Machiavelli on Modern Leadership
Tocqueville on American Character
Freedom Betrayed
Superpower Dilemmas
D'Annunzio: The First Duce
Perilous Statecraft
Debacle: Carter and the Fall of the Shah
Italy in Crisis
Universal Fascism
West European Communism and American Foreign Policy

ACCOMPLICE TO EVIL

Iran and the War Against the West

MICHAEL A. LEDEEN

TRUMAN TALLEY BOOKS
ST. MARTIN'S PRESS NEW YORK

 Printed in the United States of America. For information, address St. Martin's Press, 175 Fifth Avenue, New York, N.Y. 10010.

www.stmartins.com

Library of Congress Cataloging-in-Publication Data

Ledeen, Michael Arthur, 1941–
Accomplice to evil : Iran and the war against the West / Michael A. Ledeen.—1st ed.
p. cm.
Includes index.
ISBN 978-0-312-57069-9
1. United States—Foreign relations—Iran. 2. Iran—Foreign relations—United States. 3. Western countries—Foreign relations—Iran. 4. Iran—Foreign relations—Western countries. 5. Iran—Politics and government—1997 6. Islam and politics—Iran. 7. Terrorism—Religious aspects—Islam. 8. World politics—20th century. I. Title.
E183.8.I55L419 2009
327.73055—dc22

2009016598

First Edition: October 2009

10 9 8 7 6 5 4 3 2 1

CONTENTS

ACKNOWLEDGMENTS

Many thanks to my colleagues at the Foundation for the Defense of Democracies, notably Clifford May, Mark Dubowitz, Andy McCarthy, Claudia Rosett, and Walid Phares, for their indulgence, helpful comments, and encouragement. FDD is a wonderful place to work, and I'm fortunate to be there.

Special thanks to Nick Guariglia, who did much of the research, and to Cara Rosenthal, who did much of the thankless work that goes into a book, including the hunt for typos.

This book began under the editorial guidance of Truman Talley, and bears his imprint. Alas, it is the last I shall do with him, for he has retired. The world of letters is diminished by his departure, and I hope he enjoys the many benefits of relaxation and a charming new wife. This project concludes with the guidance of George Witte, whose suggestions have, I think, made it a better book. I look forward to future collaborations. This marks five consecutive books with St. Martin's Press, and I am most grateful.

Some of the material herein has appeared in my online writing, both in National Review Online and in Pajamas Media, where my blog "Faster, Please" appears. Many thanks to my friends Katherine Lopez and Roger Simon for giving me the chance to develop my thoughts, and to the scores of friendly and unfriendly critics who commented on the earlier efforts.

The most demanding critics of my work are Barbara and the kids, who are now writers themselves. All three children have published their own work, and no doubt will continue to do it, as they should. Honest criticism is rare, and to have it wrapped in love is unique.

Ours is now a military family. Simone has spent many months in Iraq and Afghanistan for the Defense and Treasury Departments, Gabriel was twice deployed to Anbar Province with the Marine Corps, and Daniel is now a 2nd Lieutenant in the Marines. It's an honor to have such children, as to have a wife such as Barbara, who gets up every morning knowing that the fight against evil will not end in this lifetime, and who is prepared to fight all day long. It's a blessing and a wonderment to be their father and husband, and *Accomplice to Evil* is dedicated to them all.

[The Devil] avowed to me that he had been afraid, relatively as to his proper power, once only, and that was on the day when he had heard a preacher, more subtle than the rest of the human herd, cry in his pulpit: "My dear brethren, do not ever forget, when you hear the progress of Enlightenment praised, that the loveliest trick of the Devil is to persuade you that he does not exist!"

—Baudelaire, "The Generous Gambler"

INTRODUCTION

On April 12, 1945, America's top generals—Eisenhower, Bradley, and Patton—entered Nazi death camps for the first time. They stopped first in Ohrdruf, which was one of the constellation of smaller camps that gassed some victims and sent others on to the larger facilities at Buchenwald, a few miles down the road.

The terrible secret of Hitler's program to exterminate all the European Jews—along with others, such as homosexuals and Gypsies—was well known to the American commanding officers. They had received detailed intelligence reports on the Final Solution for years, and they had read press accounts as well, such as the one in *The New York Times* the previous December, in which reporter Milton Bracker described the abandoned site of a camp at Natzweiler-Struthof. "The sturdy green barrack buildings looked exactly like those that housed forestry trainees in the United States during the early New Deal," he wrote, but those nice buildings contained rooms with S-shaped hooks attached to rods on the ceiling, from which prisoners were hung by their wrists until they were gassed to death.

Eisenhower, Bradley, and Patton undoubtedly felt they were well prepared for what they were about to see. But they weren't.

As they entered, they found corpses in striped uniforms. Some were still alive, and one of them welcomed the Americans and had begun to show them around when a Polish prisoner struck him with a slab of wood and promptly stabbed him to death. Their tour guide had actually been a camp guard masquerading as a prisoner.

As they proceeded, they found more than three thousand dead bodies, all stark naked, uncovered in their shallow graves. They entered a shed in which dead bodies had been stacked right up to the ceiling. The smells were overpowering, especially in the barracks containing barely living prisoners who, unable to move, had befouled themselves. The famously tough General Patton could not bear it; he went outside to throw up.

Like Patton, Eisenhower had been engaged in the war from North Africa to Germany. As much as anyone in the West, he had heard and read accounts of the Nazi Holocaust, and yet all that information failed to prepare him for what he saw with his own eyes. He wrote back to Washington, "from my own personal observation, I can state unequivocally that all written statements up to now do not paint the full horrors."[1]

You just had to see it. Otherwise, you could not imagine it. Accordingly, Eisenhower called on his civilian superiors to organize congressional missions to the camps, so that they could better grasp the nature of the evil we had finally defeated. And he ordered his men to film and photograph the horrors he had seen.

Even the victims were unable to recognize their doom. As the Nazi armies were closing in on Turin, Italy, members of the tiny Italian resistance went door-to-door in the Jewish neighborhoods, both in the city and local towns, urging the residents to get out of the city and take refuge in the countryside. One of them, Rabbi Augusto Segre, later recalled that it was virtually impossible to convince the Jews of Turin to seek safe haven.

> The order to arrest the Jews was given on the radio the evening of the first of December 1943. The arrests began on the second. The Jews of Asti were gathered together . . . in the center of the city. They were even permitted to leave, but with the obligation of returning before nightfall. . . . Not only did it not pass through anyone's mind to try to flee, but even those who . . . had not been arrested . . . gave themselves up of their own accord. . . . [2]

Instead of seeking safety, the Jews of Asti took up a collection to buy off the Nazi troops. Segre asked the terrible question: "Is it possible to imagine Jews giving themselves up to the Germans spontaneously, offering a certain sum, and asking to be left alone?"

Yes, it was. Even though, by 1943, everyone "knew" of the death camps, the Jews of Asti insisted on believing it would not happen to them. This was Italy, not Germany, after all. Such things didn't happen in Italy. In the end, perhaps five or ten percent of them escaped. The rest were shipped off to Auschwitz and other such extermination centers. Almost all of them were murdered.

So it was that Jewish victims and American generals failed to understand the nature of their enemies. The process of understanding unfolded over the following decades, first at the Nuremberg trials, later at the Eichmann trial, and in scores of scholarly works, autobiographies, and movies. The judges at the trials, the authors of the books, and the writers, directors, and producers of the films were driven by a passionate desire to understand how mass genocide, terror states, and global war came about—and how we can prevent them in the future.

It hasn't succeeded. Just as Hitler and Stalin declared their intention to destroy the West and impose a new tyranny on the whole world, so today the Iranian mullahs make similar statements. Just as the fascists and Communists relentlessly expanded their military power and attacked their neighbors, Iran does the same thing today. But with the exception of the Iranian nuclear program, very little attention has been paid to the nature of the regime and its murderous activities, both against the Iranian people and against the "satanic forces" the mullahs have designated as their prime targets: America, the Christian West, the Jews, and Israel. And, with the exception of some economic and financial sanctions, which very few experts believe will force the Iranians to change their behavior or the nature of the regime, no effective strategy has been designed to confront the Iranian evil.

Ever since the Second World War, we have sought answers to several basic questions: Why did the West fail to see the coming of the catastrophe? Why were there so few efforts to thwart the fascist tide, and why did virtually all Western leaders—and so many Western intellectuals—treat the fascists as if they were normal political leaders, instead of the virulent revolutionaries they really were? Why did the main designated victims—the Jews—similarly fail to recognize the magnitude of their impending doom? Why was resistance so rare?

This was not a purely academic exercise. As Marx once said, the philosophers wanted to understand the world, but the point, after all, was to change it. The study of evil is always linked to policy, whether of nation-states or individual human beings, and the point of understanding the nature of evil is to be better able to see it coming again, and fight it effectively in the future. The slogan "never again" did not mean there would never again be evil in our world; it meant that we would not again stand aside as its power grew. We would see it early, and fight it before it became a global menace.

Why did we not see it coming? And why do we not see it today, when the Islamic Republic of Iran has declared war on us, and is waging it around the world? In the case of fascism, most scholars eventually embraced a twofold explanation: the uniqueness of the evil, and the lack of historical precedent for it. How could Western leaders, let alone the victims, be blamed for failing to see something that was almost totally new—systematic mass murder on a vast scale, and a threat to civilization itself? Never before had there been such an organized campaign to destroy an entire "race," and it was therefore almost impossible to see it coming, or even to recognize it as it got under way.

Moreover, fascism emerged in the most unlikely countries on the most unlikely continent: Europe, where politics, by and large, was the heir to the Enlightenment. Most Europeans believed man was perfectible, and progress toward greater freedom and tolerance was inevitable. Italy and Germany were two of the most civilized and cultured countries in Europe, and it was difficult to appreciate that a great evil was taking control of the nations that had produced Kant, Beethoven, Dante, and Rossini. It was even more difficult to recognize that the fascists believed they were destined to dominate the world.

Therefore, it was argued, it was only logical for us to systematically refuse to see our enemies plain. Hitler's rants, whether in *Mein Kampf* or at Nazi party rallies, were often downplayed, or explained away, as merely a way of maintaining popular support. They were rarely taken seriously as solemn promises he fully intended to fulfill. Mussolini's call for the creation of a new Italian Empire, and his later alliance with Hitler, were often downplayed as mere bluster, or even excused on the grounds that, since other European countries had overseas territories, why not Italy?

Similar answers were offered when the same questions were asked about Communism a generation or two afterward. Like the Third Reich, Stalin's Soviet empire systematically murdered millions of people and Communism's messianic ambitions similarly threatened the West. Just as with fascism, most contemporaries found it nearly impossible to believe that the Gulag Archipelago was what it was. The horrors of the Soviet concentration camps only began to be recognized in the 1970s, with the publication of Aleksandr Solzhenitsyn's books (earlier works were generally ignored). Just as with fascism, we were eventually compelled to fight a world war (albeit a cold war) against it. And as with fascism, we studied it so that the next time we would see evil early enough to prevent it from threatening us again.

By now, there is very little we do not know about such regimes and such movements. Some of our greatest scholars have described them, analyzed the reasons for their success, and chronicled the wars we fought to defeat them. Our understanding is considerable, as is the honesty and intensity of our desire that such things to be prevented.

We know, in horrible detail, that the twentieth century was the bloodiest in history. Never before were so many killed on the battlefield, in extermination camps, on death marches, in reeducation centers, in prisons, and sometimes in the streets of some of the most cultured and civilized cities. Much of the killing was carefully planned and coolly, in some cases scientifically, managed. The carnage was so terrible that a new word, "genocide," was invented to deal with the systematic annihilation of entire peoples, from Armenians in the First World War to the tens of millions of Stalin's victims in the Soviet Union, the millions of Jews in the Second World War, the many tens of millions of Chinese under Maoist tyranny, a million Cambodians under Pol Pot, and hundreds of thousands of Africans in more recent years, from Rwanda and the Democratic Republic of the Congo to Darfur.

Evil regimes were not new in the last century, and they did not go away after the defeat of the Nazis, fascists, and Communists. They are decidedly present today, most prominently and menacingly in the Middle East. The world is simmering in the familiar rhetoric and actions of movements and regimes—from Hezbollah and al Qaeda to the Iranian Khomeinists and the Saudi Wahhabis—who swear to destroy us and others like us, and we are repeating the errors of the recent past. Like their twentieth-century predecessors, they openly proclaim their intentions, and carry them out whenever and wherever they can. Like our twentieth-century predecessors, we rarely take them seriously or act accordingly. More often than not, we downplay the implications and consequences of their words, as if they were some Islamic or Arab version of "politics," intended for internal consumption, and designed to accomplish domestic objectives.

Clearly, the explanations we gave for our failure to act in the last century were wrong. The rise of messianic mass movements is not new, and there is very little we do not know about them. Yet very few writers, and fewer political leaders, talk about Iran in the same language used about the totalitarians of the last century. Nor is there any excuse for us to be surprised at the success of evil leaders, even in countries with long histories and great cultural and political accomplishments. We know all about that. Iran has a great cultural and political history, far older than Italy's or Germany's or Russia's. Today, Iran has abandoned those fine traditions in favor of a brutal and fanatical regime that oppresses the Iranian people and menaces us. Yet we are largely silent about the nature and the proclaimed mission of the Tehran regime.

So we need to ask the old questions again. Why are we failing to see the mounting power of evil enemies? Why do we treat them as if they were normal politicians, as Western leaders do when they embrace negotiations as the best course of action in dealing with a regime that daily calls for our annihilation?

The short answer is Baudelaire's. We comfort ourselves with happy thoughts about human nature, and we fall prey to the Devil's trick of fooling us into believing that he doesn't exist.

This dangerous conceit usually takes the form of the deep-seated Enlightenment beliefs that all people are basically the same, all are basically good, and we're making good progress to the ideal society. Machiavelli knew better: "Man is more inclined to do evil than to do good" is the starting point for his statecraft. Most human history, above all the history of the last century, points in that direction. But we reject the evidence. It is very unpleasant to accept the fact that many people are evil, and that entire cultures, even the finest, can fall prey to evil leaders and march in lockstep to their murderous commands. Much of contemporary Western culture is deeply committed to a belief in the basic goodness of all mankind; we are reluctant to abandon that reassuring article of faith. Despite all the evidence to the contrary, we prefer to pursue the path of reasonableness, even with enemies whose thoroughly unreasonable fanaticism is manifest.

To acknowledge the Iranian threat to us means—short of a policy of national suicide—acting against it. We have all seen videos of thousands of Iranians in the streets of Tehran, led by the ruling mullahs in chants of "death to America." What do you think they mean? After the past hundred years, any prudent policy maker must assume that they mean precisely that: death to us. Yet the American discussion of the Islamic Republic of Iran does not often touch on that unpleasant fact; instead, it focuses on the mullahs' nuclear project, about which there is very little we are likely to do. And even the discussion of the Iranians' program to build atomic bombs neatly avoids dealing with those chants of "death to America," as if we were not an intended target.

Acknowledging the existence and actions of evil enemies means accepting that we are at war, and then designing and conducting a strategy to win. It means that, temporarily at least, we have to make sacrifices on many fronts: in the comforts of our lives, indeed in lives lost; in the domestic focus of our passions—careers derailed and personal freedoms subjected to unpleasant and even dangerous restrictions; and in the diversion of wealth from self-satisfaction to the instruments of power. All of this is painful; even the contemplation of it hurts.

In an eerie echo of the last century, anti-Semitism is a central theme in the vision of our current enemies. Old Jew-hating texts like *The Protocols of the Elders of Zion,* now in Farsi and Arabic, are proliferating throughout the Middle East. Calls for the destruction of the Jews appear regularly on Iranian, Egyptian, Saudi, and Syrian television, and are heard in European and American mosques. There is little if any condemnation from the West, and virtually no action against it—suggesting, at a minimum, a familiar Western indifference to the fate of the Jews.

Finally, there is the nature of Western democratic politics. None of the democracies adequately prepared for war before it was unleashed on them in the 1940s. None was prepared for the terror assault of the twenty-first century. It is very difficult for elected leaders—even those rare men and women who see what is happening and want to act—to take timely, prudent measures before full-scale war is upon them. Winston Churchill was relegated to the opposition, and became an object of widespread ridicule until the battle was unavoidable. Franklin Delano Roosevelt had to fight desperately to win a one-vote congressional approval for a national military draft a few months before Pearl Harbor.

As in the recent past, the initiative unfortunately lies with the West's enemies. Even today, when we are fighting on the battlefields of Iraq and Afghanistan, there is little apparent recognition that we are under attack by a familiar sort of enemy, and great reluctance to act accordingly. This time, ignorance cannot be claimed as an excuse. If we are defeated, it will be because of failure of will, not lack of understanding. As, indeed, was almost the case with our near-defeat in the 1940s.

The structure of this book follows the way I arrived at my conclusions. The first chapter gives several examples of our refusal to see evil, not because it was hard to see, but because we didn't want to see it. The second chapter explores why we don't want to see it (there are many reasons), with special attention to Iran. The third chapter lays out the nature of the evil we need to see today (it turns out to be surprisingly similar to the evils we refused to see in the past). The final chapter suggests the best way to defeat our Iranian enemy.

This book was written many months before the dramatic events in Iran that began on the evening of June 12, 2009, but it explains those events in considerable detail. The revolutionary insurrection had been simmering for years, and both the challenge to the regime and the brutal repression that followed had been prepared well in advance. All of this is extensively documented in the pages of this book.

Rarely has any analysis been confirmed so abundantly. *Accomplice to Evil* not only anticipated events in Iran, but also the deliberate refusal by the West, and above all the United States, to acknowledge the evil for what it was, and act accordingly. As before, the evil was right in front of our noses. And as before, we did nothing to thwart it. The Iranian victims thus joined the European Jews, and the peoples of Cambodia, Rwanda, Cuba, China, the Soviet empire, Venezuela, and other Iranian allies in South and Central America, as innocents abandoned to their unhappy fate by those who could have saved many of them. As before, the West did not lift a finger to save the Iranian people, even though much could and should have been done.

I wrote *Accomplice to Evil* in the hope that this generation of Americans will be spared the horrible experiences of Eisenhower, Patton, and Bradley, who, in the ruins of Nazi Germany, finally came face-to-face with the evil they had been fighting, and were shocked at how little they had known. They did not really understand it until they walked into the death camp at Ohrdruf. I hope that our children do not have to ask, as I asked my own parents, how could we not have known? And why did we do nothing for so long?

What will we say?

1

SEE NO EVIL, SPEAK NO EVIL

[State Department officials] have not only failed to facilitate the obtaining of information concerning Hitler's plans to exterminate the Jews of Europe but in their official capacity have gone so far as to surreptitiously attempt to stop the obtaining of information concerning the murder of the Jewish population of Europe.

—January 1944 memorandum by U.S. Treasury Department officials entitled "On the Acquiescence of this Government in the Murder of the Jews."

THE HOLOCAUST

The refusal to see evil, and the deliberate denial of its existence, are very common, whether among policy makers, intellectuals, or reporters. The most famous case is the rise of fascism and Nazism, and the consequent mass murder of the European Jews, Gypsies, Slavs, homosexuals, and other "inferior peoples." Despite the enormous literature on the Holocaust, it is still difficult to understand the determined resistance in Western capitals and leading newspapers (including *The New York Times*[1]) to believe what was happening, let alone try to do something to save the victims.

Hitler's intentions could hardly have been clearer. His racist doctrine was spelled out in *Mein Kampf*, he reiterated it in all his major speeches both before and after his seizure of power, and he acted on it in many ways, moving the Jews out of entire sectors of German life, forcing them to wear special clothes, and then moving them out of German cities.

Very few leaders were willing to see it for what it was, even though it was obvious enough, from the very first. Kristallnacht, the night in 1938 when the Nazis unleashed a wave of physical violence against German Jews and their enterprises, was well reported and well understood. From that moment, it should have been impossible for anyone to close his eyes to the fact that Hitler fully intended to annihilate the Jews of Germany, and eventually everywhere else that he could reach. *The New York Times,* which had a very mixed record on reporting the events of the Holocaust, described it on the front page in language that could not be misunderstood:

> A wave of destruction, looting and incendiarism unparalleled in Germany since the Thirty Years War and in Europe generally since the Bolshevist Revolution swept over . . . Germany today as National Socialist cohorts took vengeance on Jewish shops, offices . . .

Nonetheless, great debates raged over the meaning of the word "elimination." Yes, it was said, Hitler promised to eliminate the Jews, but that didn't mean he intended to kill them. Some chose to interpret that as a simple desire to get them out of Germany, and there were several plans to relocate Jews to Africa, as well as the long-standing "homeland" in Palestine created by the Balfour Declaration.

So there was plenty of wiggle room for Western leaders, and for the most part they wiggled until the sight of the Nazi gallows concentrated their minds on the real threat. Until then, they preferred to deny what was clearly in front of their eyes and noses.

As Robert Conquest says,

> The true criticism of Neville Chamberlain is that he could not really imagine a man like Hitler or a party like the Nazis. . . . The notion that people who raised the alarm about Hitler in the 1930s were being immoderate and unreasonable was found in the *Times* and at All Souls, in all the blinkered and complacent crannies of the Establishment. The concept of a quite different set of motivations, based on a different political psychology, was absent.[2]

But once Nazi armies started to march, it was obvious that he wanted the elimination of the Jews from every area under German control. Everywhere the Nazis went, the Jews were rounded up and shipped out. Even then, the facts were frequently denied.

By the second half of 1942, it was pretty clear that "elimination" meant physical destruction. As Walter Laqueur and Richard Breitman note,[3] a German railway officer commented that "Auschwitz surely must have become one of the biggest cities in Europe: so many people entered it, and no one ever left!" And in fact, the year before, a brave German industrialist named Eduard Schulte had learned about the Führer's orders to commence the Holocaust. In July 1942, Heinrich Himmler, the head of the SS, had gone there to watch 449 Dutch Jews gassed. Schulte got the information and carried it to Switzerland, where he gave it to Jewish leaders, the most effective of whom was Gerhardt Riegner, of the minuscule World Jewish Congress (WJC). Riegner in turn passed it on to British and American consular officers in Geneva, asking that it be given both to high officials in Washington and to the WJC head, Rabbi Steven Wise.

Schulte was a proven source. He had previously passed on accurate information about German diplomatic and military operations, demonstrating both his reliability and his access to high levels of the Nazi regime. But the Americans didn't want to hear about it. By the time the information reached the State Department, it was already wrapped in dismissive language.

The American diplomats were annoyed at being asked to deliver a private message, even though some of them understood that, given the sensitivity of the information, it made sense to use coded cables rather than the public telegraph office. But they would have nothing to do with it. The European Bureau at Foggy Bottom called the report a "war rumor inspired by fear [another memo referred to "Jewish fears"] and what is commonly understood to be the actually miserable condition of those refugees. . . ."

Schulte's information sat in the European Bureau. Roosevelt didn't see it.

Nonetheless, FDR must have known about the Nazi program to destroy the Jews. Churchill understood it from the outset, and a year before Schulte's first-hand account reached Switzerland, British intelligence had intercepted German SS transmissions about the "mass murder of Jews in every captured town and village" as the war unfolded. In August, Churchill was confident enough to say on the radio that "whole districts are being exterminated" in conquered Russian areas. It was "a crime without a name."[4]

Churchill continued to talk about Nazi crimes, despite the Americans' reluctance to push the issue or take any action on behalf of the victims. At about the same time Schulte learned about the gassing of the Dutch Jews in Auschwitz, Churchill had sent a message to a big Jewish meeting in Madison Square Garden in New York, in which he said that the Nazis had killed more than one million Jews, and that "Hitler apparently will not be satisfied until the cities of Europe in which Jews live are turned into giant cemeteries."[5] Those words were published on page four of the leading newspaper in Switzerland, the *Neue Zuricher Zeitung*. And if Churchill knew it, Roosevelt must have known it, too.

Over the course of the next several months, Rabbi Wise and other American Jewish leaders tried desperately to convince Washington policy makers that the information was accurate, and that something should be done. The diplomats resisted, arguing that "if the State Department confirmed the news it would 'come under pressure to do something.'"[6] And they were not at all inclined to recommend any action that might, they said (and would continue to say), undermine the war effort.

At the beginning of the second week in December 1942, there was a meeting with the president, at which Wise finally presented Schulte's information. No doubt Wise believed he was bringing real news to the White House, since he could not imagine that FDR—a personal friend—would remain silent if he knew the facts. In the event, Roosevelt was not surprised in the least. We knew it, he said. The problem was what, if anything, could be done about it?

In other words, Roosevelt was not going to go public about the destruction of the European Jews. When he was publicly asked about it, as at a press conference on August 21, 1942, he danced around the matter. "We want news—from any source that is reliable—of the continuation of atrocities," he said. As if he didn't have it already. Indeed, he didn't need Schulte's report, or Churchill's intercepts. All he had to do was read *The New York Times* on December 4, four days before the meeting with

Wise and the other Jewish leaders. The headline on the front page was explicit: "Two-thirds of Jews in Poland Held Slain." The *Times* reported that a million and a quarter Polish Jews were still alive, of an original population of three and a half million. But Roosevelt was still looking for reliable sources, and his diplomats were still pretending either that we did not know about it all, or that such information as we had was insufficiently documented.

Later in the month, the Americans had to be pressured by the Brits and eleven others (including eight governments-in-exile and de Gaulle's French National Committee) to sign on to a public statement that clearly described and condemned what they called "this bestial policy of cold-blooded extermination" of "hundreds of thousands of innocent men, women and children." The Americans reluctantly signed it, after losing editorial battles that would have made the statement less damning (the State Department wanted to modify "crimes" by putting "alleged" in front of it, for example). The final declaration was explicit and detailed: "None of those taken away are ever heard of again. . . . The infirm are left to die of exposure and starvation or are deliberately massacred in mass executions." The thirteen nations promised that those guilty of such crimes would be tracked down and brought to justice.[7]

Nor were American Jewish leaders particularly energetic in pressuring the Roosevelt administration to act on behalf of their dying brethren in Europe. A colleague of Wise's wrote angrily in December 1942, ". . . what are you going to do about it? . . . Why do you expose our memories to be spat upon by future generations because we acquiesced in the crime of inaction in such a time and did not try everything, I say everything in the world?"

But Wise's organization was tiny, and although he was predictably thwarted, in fact he was one of the more active advocates of action. The most effective public campaign came in 1943 from journalist Ben Hecht and supporters in the entertainment business, and it succeeded in the face of vigorous opposition from the government and from major Jewish organizations.

Hecht wrote a pageant, meant to be staged in theaters, called "We Will Never Die," that dramatized the contributions of Jews to Western civilization, and their current plight at the hands of the Nazis. It was spectacular in every sense, from a cast of hundreds to the oversized set, featuring two tablets of the Ten Commandments reaching forty feet in height. The closing scene consisted of fifty rabbis, refugees from Europe, chanting the Kaddish, the Hebrew prayer for the dead.

Official Jewish opposition was based on numerous factors, ranging from a quite legitimate fear of provoking open anti-Semitism in America to long-standing divisions (both political and religious) within the Jewish community. The Roosevelt administration opposed it because they were opposed to increased numbers of Jewish refugees (a view shared by the Brits, who were opposed to letting large numbers of Jews into Palestine for fear of antagonizing the Arabs), and because it challenged the president's policy of "rescue through victory," which effectively postponed any positive action until the war was won.

Hecht and his coproducer, Peter Bergson, finally got support from Hollywood and Broadway stars, from Kurt Weill (who wrote the music), Moss Hart (who directed it), and an array of famous actors from Paul Muni, Sylvia Sidney, and Ralph Bellamy to Burgess Meredith and Luther Adler. It was staged first in Madison Square Garden in early March, then across the country from Washington, Boston, Philadelphia, and Chicago to the Hollywood Bowl, where ten thousand people attended in mid-July.

Unlike the private approaches to the Roosevelt administration, the dramatic nationwide campaign actually had a considerable effect. Eleanor Roosevelt attended the show in Washington, and devoted one of her regular newspaper columns to it, openly sympathizing with the plight of the Jews. Such writing, and the coverage of the performances, brought the facts of the unfolding Holocaust to millions of American newspaper readers, for many of whom it was news.

Hecht and Bergson got lucky on timing: In the midst of the grand tour, British and American diplomats met in Bermuda to work out a common policy on the rapidly expanding population of Jewish refugees. After twelve days of deep thinking and animated debate, the delegates announced failure. The State Department wasn't prepared to open our doors to more refugees, and the men from Whitehall wouldn't listen to any scheme that would increase the Jewish population of Palestine.

By contrast, Bergson and Hecht argued that there were many steps the American government could take right away to save Jews from Hitler, steps that would not interfere with the war effort. For example, empty supply ships returning from Europe could be used to bring refugees who could be held in temporary detention camps. Or pressure could be put on countries such as Hungary, Romania, and Bulgaria, which were not yet occupied by the Nazis, to let their Jews emigrate. Later, the Bergson group would call for additional steps, such as bombing Auschwitz and other Nazi death camps. This was too much, even for the quiescent American Jewish community, which denounced the Bermuda charade (the *Jewish Frontier* said the diplomats behaved "in the spirit of undertakers") and pushed for congressional action.

In early autumn, the Senate Foreign Relations Committee approved a call for a new agency to rescue Jewish refugees, and hearings in the House of Representatives yielded a State Department official who drastically overstated the number that had already entered the country, thus adding impetus to the campaign.

It soon became obvious that the bill would pass both houses, and FDR judged it politically advantageous to take the action by himself, without waiting for the vote. He was no doubt encouraged to take the step after the damning Treasury Department report on the State Department's deliberate efforts to spike information about the European catastrophe. Roosevelt accordingly created the War Refugee Board in January 1944, which probably saved more than two hundred thousand lives and gave badly needed support to the heroic efforts of Raoul Wallenberg in Sweden.

Even so, it was a feeble reed in the terrible storm. On March 2, 1944, *The New York Times* ran a story from London on page four, reporting on the latest developments in Parliament. The British had created their own committee on refugees, and appropriated fifty thousand pounds to fund its efforts. But the real news came a bit further down:

> . . . S. S. Silverman, Labor member, read a report from the Jewish National Committee operating somewhere in Poland, saying:
>
> "Last month we still reckoned the number of Jews in the whole territory of Poland as from 250,000 to 300,000. In a few weeks no more than 50,000 of us will remain. In our last moment before death, the remnants of Polish Jewry appeal for help to the whole world. May this, perhaps our last voice from the abyss, reach the ears of the whole world."

This was not worth a headline, let alone placement on the front page. By then, the *Times* was telling its reporters in Europe, "Our readers are tired of horror stories. Cable only those of death tolls unusually large or deaths themselves unusually gruesome." Any reporter worth his inkwell could have sent dozens of such cables, but the editors didn't really mean it. When Raymond

Arthur Davies, a *Times* reporter in Eastern Europe, tried to do it, they wrote back: "Jewish atrocity stories are not acceptable news material."[8]

The State Department's experts could hardly have done better.

The practice of covering up Nazi atrocities was not limited to the State Department, or even to the annihilation of non-Americans. General Eisenhower ordered the documentation of the horrors of the Third Reich, but other American military officers imposed strict censorship on American soldiers who survived Nazi concentration camps. They were ordered to sign an affidavit denying they had ever had such experiences.

> [Anthony Acevedo] was one of 350 U.S. soldiers held at . . . a satellite camp of the Nazis' notorious Buchenwald concentration camp. The soldiers, working 12-hour days, were used by the German army to dig tunnels and hide equipment in the final weeks of the war. Less than half of the soldiers survived their captivity and a subsequent death march . . . [9]

Soldiers like Acevedo were warned that they could not write or speak about their suffering. The affidavit they signed flatly stated "you must give no account of your experience in books, newspapers, periodicals, or in broadcasts or in lectures." The army claimed this was necessary "to protect escape and evasion techniques and the names of personnel who helped POW escapees," but the explanation isn't convincing. The vast majority of the survivors of Buchenwald didn't escape. They were liberated by the 6th Armored Division of Patton's Third Army. There was certainly no need to protect the names of the American liberators.

The same vow of silence was imposed on the survivors of the Bataan Death March and subsequent imprisonment, slave labor, torture, and execution that killed off nine of every ten Americans captured by the Japanese.

THE BETRAYAL OF AMERICAN POWS

Similarly, aside from occasional spasms of public interest, and exemplary research carried out by a military commission and the Senate Foreign Relations Committee, surprisingly little attention has been paid to the crimes of the Soviet Union, including the fate of thousands of Americans who vanished into the Communist prison-camp system throughout the twentieth century. From the Bolshevik Revolution until the end of the Cold War, the Soviets repeatedly captured or kidnapped American military personnel, diplomats (some of whom may have been working under cover for the intelligence community), and even ordinary citizens. Some of them were eventually released (usually as part of a swap for Soviet spies or POWs held by the United States), some vanished, and others were executed. According to one report from an important Czech military defector (General Jan Sejna, who testified on these matters in 1996), some were subjected to medical experiments in North Korea and the Soviet Union, a grim replay of the ones carried out in the Nazi death camps. After the end of the Cold War, the Joint Commission Support Directorate-Moscow (which pored through Soviet documents) issued a government report[10] that summarized it,

> Americans, including American servicemen, were imprisoned in the former Soviet Union. The Soviets and their Warsaw Pact allies even transferred some of these Americans from satellite states such as the German Democratic Republic to the Soviet Union, where they were detained.

This report, known as "The Gulag Study," details case after case, from Lenin's day through the Vietnam War.

According to a Senate report,[11] "Soviet and Asian Communist regimes view POW/MIAs, living or dead, not as a problem of humanitarian concern, but as leverage for political bargaining, as an involuntary source of technical assistance [a euphemism for interrogation, frequently under torture], and as forced labor." To which Henry Holzer, a distinguished American jurist, adds two other motives: to obtain hard cash and needed goods, and to turn them into human guinea pigs.

The pattern started very early. *The New York Times* reported on April 18, 1921, that Americans held by the Soviets included one Demetrius Kalimatian, an employee of the American embassy in St. Petersburg. The Soviets offered to release him in exchange for the freedom of American Socialist leader Eugene Debs, then in prison. Debs's sentence was commuted by President Harding. The *Times* added that during the Wilson presidency, the Soviets threatened to murder Americans under their control unless "Russian Bolsheviki held in the United States under the Espionage Law were released."

In the fall of 1921, the U.S. and Russia signed the Riga agreement, which called for American aid to the Soviet Union, and the Soviets would release all Americans in the USSR. The Americans expected twenty-one to be released. A hundred were turned over.

In like manner, the Soviets started taking American hostages late in the Second World War. In early 1945, our ambassador to Moscow, Averill Harriman, cabled FDR to say that "there appear to be hundreds of our prisoners wandering about Poland trying to locate American contact officers for protection. I am told that our men don't like the idea of getting into a Russian camp."

Six days later Ambassador Harriman sent another cable to

Washington, this time to the Secretary of State, Edward R. Stettinius, Jr.:

> [T]he Soviet Government is trying to use our liberated prisoners of war as a club to induce us to give increased prestige to the Provisional Polish Government by dealing [directly] with it in this connection. . . .

Soviet documents showed that the same practice took place on an even larger scale during the Korean War. *Newsweek* wrote in its June 19th, 2000, issue that "hundreds" of American POWs ended up in the Gulag.

> . . . the Kremlin's archives yielded an extraordinary exchange of telegrams among Joseph Stalin, [Chinese Communist Foreign Minister] Zhou Enlai and the North Korean strongman Kim Il Sung. . . . Toward the end of the war, the Chinese suggested that if American prisoners were to be repatriated, "at least 20 percent should be held back." Mao thought he could use the prisoners as political pawns . . . to win a U.N. seat and diplomatic recognition.

It never occurred to the Soviets that there was anything wrong with using American prisoners—or anyone else, including their own citizens—as political pawns. For them, the interests of the state were paramount, and questions of human rights were irrelevant. The Soviets unhesitatingly lied to American officials, including several presidents, and yet subsequent generations of Americans acted as if Russian dictators were basically honest, and shared our view of proper behavior.

Delusions persisted about the nature of the Soviet Union and its leaders, including Stalin. As Robert Conquest puts it,

> The delusive view of the Soviet phenomenon to be found in Western intellectual, or near intellectual, circles in the 1930s, and to some extent again in the first postwar decade and later, will be incredible to later students of mental aberration.[12]

THE BETRAYAL OF RUSSIAN ANTICOMMUNIST POWS

This delusion contributed to one of the most dreadful events in the immediate aftermath of the Second World War, when the leaders of our "great generation" (in tandem with our British allies) sent between two million and three million Soviet citizens back to almost certain death, torture, or misery. Some were soldiers and officers, and some of those had joined the Nazi armies and fought against us and the Russians. Others were innocent civilians who had become conscripted slaves of the Third Reich. Still others, like the Cossacks, were enemies of the Bolshevik regime who had long lived in the West and had seized the opportunity to fight the Soviets.

We did not distinguish among them. Stalin wanted them all back, and although many begged for asylum in the West, and although our policy violated international law and a formal undertaking from our acting secretary of state, we delivered them to him. They were executed, tortured, jailed, or shipped to the Gulag, where Aleksandr Solzhenitsyn heard their stories. He later wrote about those "civilians of all ages and of both sexes who had been fortunate enough to find shelter on Allied territory, but who in 1946–1947 were perfidiously returned by Allied authorities into Soviet hands."[13] The most famous single group thus betrayed was what Mr. Solzhenitsyn called "the Vlasov people,"named after Gen. Andrey Andreyevich Vlasov, a heroic Red Army commander who brought his million men over to the German side after being betrayed by Stalin at the battle of Leningrad in 1942.

Vlasov was driven at least in part by a lust for vengeance, but in truth the captured Russians had little choice in the matter. The Nazis would enter prisoner-of-war camps and ask for volunteers, and the first to refuse was shot on the spot. The rest were quick to seize the opportunity for a longer life, a bit of food, and a new German uniform.

At war's end, Stalin was eager to get Vlasov and his million followers into early graves, or slave camps, and we and the British were quick to accommodate him. We knew their destiny, since we knew that Stalin had defined all those who surrendered to the Germans as "traitors." Vlasov was hanged and decapitated; his severed head was displayed in Red Square. Almost all the other officers were executed, and hundreds of thousands of his followers were sent to die in the Gulag.

The case of the Cossacks was similar, but even closer to home. Thousands of Cossacks enlisted in the German army to avenge their defeat after the Russian Revolution, and many of them ended up in American POW camps in this country and in Central Europe. They fought desperately to stay in the free world. Nearly two hundred of them, held in Fort Dix, New Jersey, rioted when they were loaded onto a ship, and they literally wrecked the engine with their bare hands. Brought back to Fort Dix, they implored the Americans to shoot them on free soil. Instead we drugged them and shipped them off. As Lord Bethell wrote in his impassioned book, *The Last Secret*, "the Cossacks were not only drowning themselves, but also their children."[14]

Forced repatriation took a moral toll on Allied soldiers, and there were clear signs of rebellion, sometimes at very high levels. British field marshal Harold Alexander, for example, wrote to his political bosses that the policy was contrary to democratic principles and urged that it be changed. Gen. Dwight Eisenhower, after several months of acquiescence to Stalin's wishes, called an end to the dreadful operation.

Despite all that, and despite the heinous behavior of the Kremlin with regard to American POWs and kidnap victims in subsequent years, there was still a remarkable willingness to trust Soviet dictators, even—and in some ways, especially—Stalin.

STALIN AND MUSSOLINI

Nowhere was this better dramatized than in the reaction to the brutal murder by Soviet NKVD agents of more than twenty-five thousand Poles in the spring of 1940 in what has come to be known as the Katyn massacre. The slaughter was carried out after Stalin's troops moved into Poland, the counterpart to Hitler's invasion from the West a couple of weeks earlier (the two tyrants had just signed their strategic agreement).

The Russians immediately blamed the Germans for the massacre, and although for more than half a century there was plenty of evidence that the Soviets had done the terrible deed, it wasn't until 1989 that a Soviet military court opened a formal case and declared the massacre a genocide (only to have Putin order the case closed in 2004, and proclaim that the genocide had not been proven). And Boris Yeltsin gave the Poles a document from the Soviet Politburo archives that contained the resolution ordering the execution of ten thousand Polish POWs.

The distinguished Russian-Italian historian Victor Zaslavsky has produced a new study of Katyn which carries the chilling words

> The Soviet leadership could not have covered up its responsibility . . . if Western governments had not played along

> and done all they could to withhold information. . . . The American government persisted in this until the early 1950s, whereas the British government continued to do so right up to the collapse of the Soviet regime.[15]

The British government at least had the early excuse of not having particularly good information, and Churchill wrote Eden in late April 1943, "There is no use prowling round the three year old graves. . . ." The war was in full swing; the Soviets, having been invaded by Hitler, were now allies; and Churchill, predictably, wanted to avoid unpleasantness within the Alliance over something that was both ambiguous and a fait accompli. This laid down the pattern for the next half century.

Roosevelt's motives for accepting Soviet lies about Katyn were rather different, at once more personal and more ambitious. He rather liked the Soviet dictator, and he believed it would be necessary to have Soviet cooperation in building a stable postwar Europe. He was therefore furious when the American special envoy to the Balkans, Ambassador George Earle, sent him a thick file demonstrating the Soviets had killed tens of thousands of Poles at Katyn. Roosevelt called it "German propaganda" and pronounced himself "absolutely convinced the Russians did not do this."[16] When Earle persisted in gathering still more evidence, the president ordered him to stop, and wrote a personal note: "I specifically forbid you to publish any information or opinion about an Ally that you may have acquired while in office or in the service of the U.S. Navy." Just to make sure Earle got the message, Roosevelt arranged to have him sent to Samoa, where he warmed his heels until after FDR had died. Meanwhile, the bureaucracy was willing to participate in large-scale falsification of the historical record. In the State Department and the White House, the early equivalent of shredding went on apace. "Documents written by American officials and diplomats accusing the

Soviets of the murders were destroyed or simply made to disappear." Thus, when Arthur Bliss Lane was named ambassador to Poland in 1944, the only "information" he received about Katyn was a report that accused the Germans of doing it.

In like manner, take the case of Holodomor, the terrible famine of 1932–33, when Stalin's policies led to the starvation of millions of poor Ukrainians at the incredible rate of twenty-five thousand peasants per day. The European Parliament has proclaimed it a crime against humanity, and fourteen countries, including the United States, have branded it a genocide.

As Robert Conquest, the great historian of the Soviet Terror, has noted,[17] the deliberate and systematic decimation of the Ukrainians (and many other "nationalities" in the Soviet empire) had two terrible effects: Over the next decade or so, more than ten million peasants died. At the same time, as Bukharin bitterly remarked, the Communists who oversaw the mass murder were transformed into brutal bureaucrats for whom terror was an acceptable, normal method of carrying out "the revolution." Brutalization at the top, murder at the bottom.

It was not hard to find out what was going on, and most Western embassies reported at least the basic facts. Moreover, several newspapers and magazines (alas, all too often written off with the epithet "right wing") carried reportage from travelers in the region, and in Britain and Europe there was some excellent coverage, notably from Malcolm Muggeridge in the *Manchester Guardian* (he managed to beat the Soviet censors by smuggling some of his reports in the diplomatic pouch). Gareth Jones went unannounced from Moscow to the Ukraine (if he had asked for permission, it would not have been allowed), and once safely back home he wrote extensively about the dreadful spectacle he'd witnessed, "the swollen stomachs of the children in the cottages in which I slept," the death of 80 percent of the horses, and the constant cry: "There is no bread. We are dying."[18]

And yet, in another leitmotif of the modern world, there was a strenuous effort to deny what was going on, just as with the Holocaust. The most celebrated case is *The New York Times*'s man in Moscow, the infamous Walter Duranty, who coined the word "Stalinism," and who seems to have invented the slogan "you can't make an omelet without breaking some eggs," which has often been used to justify revolutionary violence. Malcolm Muggeridge called him "the greatest liar of any journalist I have met in fifty years of journalism,"[19] upon learning that Duranty had told his readers that "any report of a famine in Russia is today an exaggeration or malignant propaganda,"[20] but informed the British chargé d'affairs in Moscow that "the Ukraine had been bled white . . . Mr. Duranty thinks it is quite possible that as many as ten million people may have died directly or indirectly from lack of food in the Soviet Union during the past year."

Readers of the *Times* got the lies, the author of those lies was rewarded with the Pulitzer Prize, and his false reporting was hailed by *The Nation* as "the most enlightening, dispassionate and readable despatches . . . which appeared in any newspaper in the world." To this day, the *Times* refuses to give back the Pulitzer Prize Duranty was awarded for his pro-Stalin "reporting" during those dark years.

Duranty considered Stalin one of the world's greatest leaders, and he was certainly not exceptional in that. Even after Stalin's crimes had been revealed, even after the horrors of the Soviet empire had been exposed by Solzhenitsyn, Sharansky, and Bukovsky, there were still leading intellectuals who refused to condemn it. The celebrated British Marxist historian Eric Hobsbawm was one of these:

> Not long ago, on a popular television show, Hobsbawm explained that the fact of Soviet mass-murdering made no difference to his Communist commitment. In astonishment,

> his interviewer asked, "What that comes down to is saying that had the radiant tomorrow actually been created, the loss of fifteen, twenty million people might have been justified?" Without hesitation Hobsbawm replied, "Yes."[21]

Other journalists, politicians, and intellectuals felt the same way about Italy's fascist leader, Benito Mussolini. With rare exceptions, *The New York Times*'s correspondents in Rome prior to the Italian invasion of Ethiopia in the mid-thirties (almost a decade and a half after the march on Rome) were great admirers of *Il Duce*.[22] One of their reporters, Walter Littlefield, even received a medal from the Italian government, and he was not alone. His *Times* colleague Anne O'Hare McCormick defended the African invasion, Italian involvement in the Spanish Civil War, and even the alliance with Hitler. To be sure, the *Times* editorialists were more clear-eyed, and were among the first to point out the similarities between Italian fascism and the Bolshevik regime in the Soviet Union. But even so, the *Times* greatly admired Mussolini's corporate doctrine, going so far as to write, in 1925, that Mussolini's conception of power and authority "has many points in common with that of the men who inspired our own constitution—John Adams, Hamilton, and Washington. The uninformed will of 'the many' is to be 'balanced' by the experience and wisdom of 'the few.' "[23]

As John Diggins, the author of an exemplary study of American attitudes toward Mussolini's fascist state, noted,

> . . . only a small minority of American papers categorized the new government as a "dictatorship" and . . . *The New York Times* was almost alone in asserting (editorially) that the Fascists themselves were opposed to democracy. Possibly because the takeover had met so little resistance, most viewers were led to believe that the movement had the sup-

> port of the Italian masses. At least one paper, the *Cleveland Plain Dealer*, was convinced that Fascism had in fact saved democracy in Italy.[24]

Even writers from the left fell in love with Mussolini (a harbinger of the smooth transition many fascist intellectuals made to Italian communism after World War II), as did some of FDR's "brain trust." Rexford Guy Tugwell, one of Roosevelt's closest advisers, called Mussolini's fascism "the cleanest, neatest, most efficiently operating piece of social machinery I've ever seen. It makes me envious," and the great leftist muckraker, Ida Tarbell, called Mussolini "a despot with a dimple."[25]

Nor was Hollywood immune to his charms; in 1923 Lionel Barrymore starred in *The Eternal City*, an ode to the fascist March on Rome the previous year. And even American Jews hailed him; ten years later, an association of Jewish publishers declared Mussolini one of the world's twelve greatest Christian friends of the Jewish people.

In large part, the pro-fascist attitudes of so many Americans (and a large swath of the western European press as well, particularly in France and England) were generated not so much by studied approval of the course of events in Italy (those who looked hard at the mounting repression there more often than not criticized it) as by infatuation with Mussolini himself.[26] He had a magnetic personality, and he worked in one of the most beautiful and imposing buildings in Rome, the Palazzo Venezia. Having been a successful journalist himself, he knew how to appeal to his interlocutors, and he gave an amazing number of interviews to journalists and visiting dignitaries. More often than not, he swept them off their feet; Will Rogers was utterly charmed, although nothing like the mayor of Liverpool, Margaret Beavan, who described her epiphany in the *Daily Mail* at the end of May 1928:

> I have never had such an emotion in my life. I have never seen a man so different from all others, nor such a magnetic personality. He is so imposing that I don't have words to describe it. I am moved in every fibre by his dominating, magnetic, imposing, immense personality. . . .

Another foreigner who embraced Mussolini later became one of the most influential journalists of the century: an American journalist who put Fidel Castro on the front page, and perhaps in power in Havana.

CASTRO

Fidel Castro was an American hero before he became the ruler of the Cuban people, in large part because of the work of the *New York Times* journalist Herbert Matthews. In early 1957, Matthews interviewed Fidel in a mountain hideout, and he wrote a fawning interview that appeared on the front page. Two more articles followed.

Matthews's articles enraged the Cuban dictator Fulgencio Batista, who several months earlier had announced that Castro had been killed by Cuban forces. The articles helped Castro enormously, first because they portrayed him in glowing and reassuring terms (he was described as a young, charismatic democrat and a convinced friend of the American people), and second because they conveyed a totally false picture of Castro's strength; Matthews believed Castro's exaggerated claims about the number of his followers. They were three times the actual number.

Matthews's stories had an enormous effect, both on American public opinion (which shifted from support for Batista to substantial sympathy for Castro) and on American foreign policy, which eventually terminated military assistance to Batista.

Matthews was greatly pleased, and happily referred to himself as "the man who invented Fidel."

It was not the first time that Matthews had hailed a totalitarian leader. He supported Mussolini for more than a decade, and even endorsed the Italian invasion of Ethiopia. A few years later he changed his mind, and backed the Communists in the Spanish Civil War. Castro was only the latest in a series of charismatic leaders to gain Matthews's enthusiastic support. "I feel about Cuba somewhat as I did about Spain," he said, and he might well have added Italy to the list.

Matthews never apologized for any of his political enthusiasms for evil men of both left and right. He remained a Castro apologist, even in the face of the mass repression and executions carried out by the Cuban Communists, as he remained an avid supporter of the Republicans in the Spanish Civil War, even in the face of the summary executions carried out under Soviet orders. He was even unrepentant for his hero worship of *Il Duce.*

Matthews's insistence that he was right all along is not unusual; on the contrary, it's rare that anyone—or any nation—feels obliged to apologize for their blindness to, embrace of, or cooption by evil. In 1995, French president Jacques Chirac became the first French leader to publicly recognize national responsibility for the country's role in the Holocaust. Even so, it was not until 2009 that France formally acknowledged that the state itself was culpable in the deportation of Jews to the death camps.

The greater the evil, the more difficult to admit culpability. If you admit error on such a fundamental matter, it requires you to rethink all your moral and political principles—why else did you become an accomplice to evil?—and act accordingly. So it was with several generations of ex-Communists who, having broken with the party, moved to the political right. Whether it be Americans like Whittaker Chambers and Ronald Radosh,

Frenchmen like André Glucksmann and François Furet, or Italians like Enzo Bettiza and Renzo De Felice, once they recognized the evil for what it was, they reconsidered all the passions and ideas that had led them to embrace it.

Few possess the moral and intellectual courage and rigor to put themselves through this difficult and painful process. Cases like Matthews's are far more common, as we saw when Soviet Communism came crashing down in the late 1980s and early 1990s. Communist supporters (whether or not they were party members) had some difficult questions to answer, above all to themselves. In 1994, a heated debate was published in *Dissent* magazine, the flagship publication of the intellectual left.[27] The centerpiece of the debate was a fiery essay by the Marxist historian Eugene Genovese, the author of several important books on slavery and the American South.

Genovese had been a member of the American Communist Party in his youth, and was thrown out at age twenty. Nonetheless, he said, "I remained a supporter of the international movement and of the Soviet Union until there was nothing left to support." And yet, Genovese wrote in a tone of mixed surprise and accusation, nobody had called him to account. Nobody had asked him "What did you know [about the evils of Soviet Communism], and when did you know it?" But that was not the real question. "We have a disquieting number of corpses to account for," he said, and they had known it all along. Solzhenitsyn's *Gulag Archipelago* had been in print since the 1970s. Worse still, was it not true that "throughout history, from ancient times to the peasant wars of the sixteenth century to the Reign of Terror and beyond, social movements that have espoused radical egalitarianism and participatory democracy have begun with mass murder and ended in despotism"?

Why, then, had they not seen that those corpses were the result of a system they had long supported?

The responses begged the question. Some regretted their silence about the evils of the Soviet world, while others challenged one detail or another of Genovese's indictment. But none of them was prepared to reconsider his basic principles. All agreed that Stalinism was a bad thing. Some said, in essence, "I should have denounced it earlier." But no one agreed with Genovese that the horrors of Soviet Communism demanded a systematic examination of radical egalitarianism and participatory democracy, so that similar horrors could be confronted in the future. Nor were they willing to deal with the central question: Why had they not seen the evil when it was right in front of their faces?

Those on the other end of the political spectrum were equally unwilling to admit error and try to ensure the defeat of evil the next time it arose. Nazi leaders did not beg for forgiveness at Nuremburg, and Eichmann even denied he was an anti-Semite. Nor did Nazi collaborators embark upon rigorous self-criticism. Indeed, at least one celebrated collaborator still sees nothing wrong with what he did: the financier George Soros. Interviewed by Steve Kroft on CBS News's *60 Minutes,* Soros calmly insisted that his collaboration with the Nazis, wherein he became a cog in the machine that killed his fellow Hungarian Jews, was right.[28]

> When the Nazis occupied Budapest in 1944, George Soros's father was a successful lawyer. He lived on an island in the Danube and liked to commute to work in a rowboat. But knowing there were problems ahead for the Jews, he decided to split his family up. He bought them forged papers and he bribed a government official to take fourteen-year-old George Soros in and swear that he was his Christian godson. But survival carried a heavy price tag. While hundreds of thousands of Hungarian Jews were being shipped off to the death camps, George Soros accompanied his phony

godfather on his appointed rounds, confiscating property from the Jews.

(Vintage footage of Jews walking in line; man dragging little boy in line.)

KROFT: *(Voiceover)* These are pictures from 1944 of what happened to George Soros's friends and neighbors.

(Vintage footage of women and men with bags over their shoulders walking; crowd by a train.)

KROFT: *(Voiceover)* You're a Hungarian Jew . . .

SOROS: *(Voiceover)* Mm-hmm.

KROFT: *(Voiceover)* . . . who escaped the Holocaust . . .

(Vintage footage of women walking by train.)

SOROS: *(Voiceover)* Mm-hmm.

(Vintage footage of people getting on train.)

KROFT: *(Voiceover)* . . . by . . . by posing as a Christian.

SOROS: *(Voiceover)* Right.

(Vintage footage of women helping each other get on train; train door closing with people in boxcar.)

KROFT: *(Voiceover)* And you watched lots of people get shipped off to the death camps.

SOROS: Right. I was fourteen years old. And I would say that that's when my character was made.

KROFT: In what way?

SOROS: That one should think ahead. One should understand and . . . and anticipate events and when . . . when one is threatened. It was a tremendous threat of evil. I mean, it was a . . . a very personal experience of evil.

KROFT: My understanding is that you went out with this protector of yours who swore that you were his adopted godson.

SOROS: Yes. Yes.

KROFT: Went out, in fact, and helped in the confiscation of property from the Jews.

SOROS: Yes. That's right. Yes.

KROFT: I mean, that's— that sounds like an experience that would send lots of people to the psychiatric couch for many, many years. Was it difficult?

SOROS: Not . . . not at all. Not at all. Maybe as a child you don't— you don't see the connection. But it was— it created no . . . no problem at all.

KROFT: No feeling of guilt?

SOROS: No.

KROFT: For example that, "I'm Jewish and here I am, watching these people go. I could just as easily be there. I should be there." None of that?

SOROS: Well, of course I c— I could be on the other side or I could be the one from whom the thing is being taken away. But there was no sense that I shouldn't be there, because that was—well, actually, in a funny way, it's just like in markets—that if I weren't there— of course, I wasn't doing it, but somebody else would . . . would . . . would be taking it away anyhow. And it was the— whether I was there or not, I was only a spectator, the property was being

> taken away. So the— I had no role in taking away that property. So I had no sense of guilt.

Does being an accomplice to evil mean you never have to say you're sorry? Soros never even raised the moral question, even late in life. He didn't even seem to understand it. "If I hadn't done it, somebody else would," he says. For him, the question of evil simply makes no sense at all.

KENNEDY, CUBA, AND THE SOVIETS

Personal relationships matter a great deal, perhaps especially at the highest levels of international affairs. American leaders' willingness to believe the best about some very bad people has often led them to make tragic errors. John F. Kennedy, for example, came from a tough family and had fought in a war, but he was deceived by Nikita Khrushchev on a vital matter of national security, and it almost plunged the world into a nuclear war. To be sure, some of his top advisers were also wrong about Soviet intentions, but Kennedy's mistake was greatly encouraged by his misreading of Khrushchev himself.

Throughout the second year of Kennedy's presidency, the CIA repeatedly told him that he didn't have to worry about the Soviet Union putting nuclear weapons in Cuba. Such a step, the agency confidently stated in a National Intelligence Estimate on September 19, 1962, "would be incompatible with Soviet policy as we presently estimate it." The agency's conclusion was in line with the virtually unanimous view of Cuban experts, both in the United States and in allied countries. Michael Dobbs tells us[29] that "the entire Western diplomatic corps in Cuba" was of the same opinion. And JFK was personally convinced, for reasons having nothing to do with spycraft, that Khrushchev would not do such a thing at that time.

Less than a month later, on October 13, a U-2 spy plane flew over Cuba and saw the Soviet missiles there.

There had always been plenty of "evidence" that Khrushchev had ordered the deployment of nuclear missiles to Cuba. As usual, human sources had told the CIA that, and the opposite. Human intelligence (HUMINT) could justify any conclusion. Unable to sort out the reliable from the fanciful, the "signal" from the "background noise," the agency returned to basics: What made sense? The agency's top analysts couldn't imagine that the Soviets would do something so risky and so destabilizing. They couldn't believe that the Soviets truly meant to dominate the world, and were prepared to deceive the United States about their real intentions.

Moreover, Khrushchev himself had promised Kennedy—who was facing midterm elections in less than a month—that he wouldn't do anything to "embarrass the . . . president politically before the . . . elections."[30] Perhaps Khrushchev thought he'd been technically true to his word; after all, he hadn't announced his dramatic escalation of the Cold War. In any event, Khrushchev's promise reinforced the analysts' view that the Soviets would not risk nuclear escalation in the western hemisphere.

Hence the National Intelligence Estimate (NIE) language, which tacitly assumed that the Soviet dictator thought the same way as an American president.

To his credit, agency director John McCone saw things more clearly than his highly trained spooks. The Soviets had installed surface-to-air missiles all around Cuba. Why? The most straightforward explanation was that they were hiding something, and wanted to be able to shoot down American spy planes before we spotted whatever they were hiding. But the president went with the reassuring Estimate, and when the Soviet missiles were photographed by the U-2, he hit the roof.

> The news from Cuba reinforced Kennedy's impression of Khrushchev as a "f***ing liar." He complained to his brother that the Soviet leader had behaved like "an immoral gangster . . . not as a statesman, not as a person with a sense of responsibility."

There was no reason to believe that Khrushchev, or any other Soviet dictator, was a statesman with a sense of responsibility. Indeed, Kennedy had been blackmailed by the Soviet bloc after the debacle at the Bay of Pigs in 1961, when he had engineered "private humanitarian aid" to Cuba in the form of powdered milk, baby food, and medicines as ransom for the American-trained guerrillas captured by Castro's army.

Kennedy's surprise that Khrushchev—contrary to the president's own personal experience and the considered analysis of the CIA's Soviet experts—had deceived him was part of a long pattern.

American leaders have long embraced the belief that the most powerful people in the world are much like anyone else, and that an appeal to reason will yield reasonable outcomes. In case after case, American leaders refused to recognize evil when it should have been manifestly clear what we were dealing with. Tyrants like Khrushchev, Stalin, Mussolini, and Khomeini were very nasty people who had come to power by brutally crushing their opponents, and their view of statecraft was very different from the one promoted by professors of "conflict resolution" in leading American universities. Yet time and time again, policy makers, analysts, and intellectuals insisted on seeing them as "people like us," with the same desires for peace and the improvement of their citizens' lot—as democratic leaders. And time and time again, Americans and other peoples suffered or died as a result of our refusal to see evil and take timely action.

Contrary to our wishful thinking, many of the men and women who govern the destiny of our world are evil. Machiavelli is not the only sage who recognized it, but he put it most concisely and brutally: "Man is more inclined to do evil than to do good." Rational statecraft starts right there.

The American founders knew their Machiavelli: Recognizing man's innate capacity for evil, they designed a system of checks and balances to thwart the accumulation of power by any group, lest the entire enterprise fall into wicked hands. They knew the battle for liberty would never end. Benjamin Franklin famously warned we would have to fight to keep our republic.

All of this wisdom has been dangerously undermined by the foolish notion that man is basically good, that all men are basically the same, and that all we need do is to permit history to take its preordained course. These are the tenets of contemporary education. Our children, along with the rest of us, are forbidden to criticize "others," whether of different pigmentation or religion.

This vision rests on a demonstrably false vision of man. We are not naturally inclined to do good. Quite the contrary; left to our own devices, we produce genocide in Europe, Asia, and Africa. The evil spreads, oblivious to race, religion, tribe, or nation. Ask the Georgians. Ask Middle Eastern Jews and Christians, or the Iranian, Iraqi, or Syrian peoples, or the Hutus and the Tutsis, or the victims of the Darfur massacres.

RWANDA

No doubt many imagine the African genocide of the mid-1990s as a case of mob savagery, of one tribe slaughtering another in a wild bloody massacre. But in many ways, it was the African equivalent of the Nazis' methods. The whole thing was carefully organized, and the actual killing was methodical, not frenzied. Philip Gourevitch, trying to understand the Rwanda genocide, was surprised:

> [it] is tempting to play with theories of collective madness, mob mania, a fever of hatred erupted into a mass crime of passion, and to imagine the blind orgy of the mob. . . . But . . . hundreds of thousands of Hutus had worked as killers in regular shifts. There was always the next victim, and the next.[31]

It was orderly, reminiscent of the Holocaust camps (and some of the leaders of the Hutu Power movement understood that; they compared the Tutsis to the Jews). His description is echoed by the novelist Gil Courtemanche:

> In the towns both large and small, the genocide had been more systematic. Meetings had been organized, watchwords and directives had been given, plans had been laid. . . . They were too poor to build gas chambers. . . . The churches became Rwanda's gas chambers.[32]

There were United Nations "peacekeeping forces" in Rwanda, but they did next to nothing, not even to save their own comrades. When ten Belgian soldiers were beaten and killed, the UN didn't lift a finger, either to save them or to go after their killers. Nor did anyone else intervene to stop the genocide. The French government piously took the position that the Hutu majority's wishes should be respected, so the Quai d'Orsay evacuated its personnel (and a few favored Tutsis) and then stood back and watched. Debates at UN headquarters in New York were generally acrobatic balancing acts, as the diplomats danced all around the dreaded word "genocide," which would have required forceful action. The State Department never used the word. Gourevitch describes the dark humor at Foggy Bottom:

> The official formulation approved by the White House was: "Acts of genocide may have occurred." When Christine Shelley, a State Department spokeswoman, tried to defend this semantic squirm at a press briefing . . . she was asked how many acts of genocide it takes to make a genocide.[33]

The Clinton administration was resolutely opposed to doing anything, prevented the United States from having anything to do with UN peacekeeping missions, and singlehandedly made sure the UN would do nothing of consequence. Some years later, Clinton himself apologized for his administration's failure to fully realize what was happening, and to do enough to stop it. But it was the same story all over again. There was plenty of information, concerned and well-informed witnesses were begging for action, hundreds of thousands of people were being slaughtered. American leaders simply chose to ignore or downplay the evidence and stay out.[34] Thus, "whatever their convictions about 'never again,' many of them did sit around, and they most certainly did allow genocide to happen."

Gourevitch draws the obvious conclusion: "If Rwanda's experience could be said to carry any lessons for the world, it was that endangered peoples who depend on the international community for physical protection stand defenseless."

CAMBODIA

The terrible slaughter of the Cambodian people between 1975 and 1979 at the hands of Pol Pot, following the withdrawal of

American forces from the region in the second half of the 1970s, was similarly ignored or suppressed until it was too late for anything to be done to save the victims. In this case, it was not the government that closed its eyes; it was the intellectuals and reporters, many of whom had long argued that America was the source of all evil in Southeast Asia. William Shawcross was one of those, and he sadly reflected on the willful blindness that was self-inflicted by him and his colleagues. "In Indochina," he later wrote, "the majority of American and European journalists (including myself) believed the war could not or should not be won. At the end one *New York Times* headline read: 'Indochina without Americans: for most, a better life.' [The headline accompanied an upbeat report from Sidney Schanberg on April 13, 1975.] Such naivety was horribly wrong . . ."[35]

Shawcross was not the only one to ultimately recognize he had made a terrible mistake; Ben Kiernan, who later headed the excellent Cambodian Genocide Program at Yale University,[36] wrote angrily when the first reports of the massacres began to appear in the press, "the Khmer Rouge movement is not the monster that the press have recently made it out to be." Stanley Karnow said at the time that "the 'loss' of Cambodia would . . . be the salvation of the Cambodians." *The New Republic* happily announced that "the Cambodian people will finally be rescued from the horrors of a war that never really had any meaning,"[37] and academics Gareth Porter and G. C. Hildebrand of the Indochina Resource Center actually claimed that Pol Pot's policies had "saved the lives of thousands of people."

The refusal to see and report Pol Pot's mass murder was embarrassing to the journalists and scholars, but it had no immediate policy consequences. Shawcross argues that because so many American and European reporters denied the clear evidence in the 1970s, the next generation of journalists was under a special moral obligation to take great care in their reporting of the Iraq war thirty years later. He was not greatly impressed with what he saw coming out of Iraq and Afghanistan; it seemed to him that the same pattern was being repeated. The sins of America's enemies were minimized, and the errors of the Americans and their allies were exaggerated.

That was certainly the case in the matter of Iran, the subject that will occupy much of what follows.

THE AYATOLLAH KHOMEINI AND THE IRANIAN REVOLUTION

The Khomeini case was particularly egregious. The ayatollah was a sworn enemy of America, Israel, and indeed the entire non-Muslim world, especially the Baha'is and the Jews. His doctrine was published in two books of lectures, speeches, and public harangues, one (in 1970) in Arabic, the other (in 1975) in Farsi. In addition, for several years prior to the 1979 revolution that brought him to power, Khomeini had smuggled thousands of audio cassettes into Iran, where they were played in the mosques.

There was little excuse for American experts to portray Khomeini as a "moderate," a man little interested in governing, and a reformist. Anyone reading or listening to Khomeini's words had to realize that he was totally opposed to most of the values and accomplishments of contemporary Western civilization. The shah's greatest sin was his campaign to westernize Iran, a campaign Khomeini described as "the abolition of the laws of Islam."[38] Khomeini attacked element after element of modern society, from female teachers in boys' schools and male teachers in girls' schools, to appointing lay persons to key positions in the judicial system, by which, in Khomeini's words, "the government's Ministry of Justice has shown its opposition to . . . Islam. From this point on, Jews, Christians, and enemies of Islam and of the Muslims must interfere in the affairs of Muslims." The laxity of the courts was anathema to the ayatollah. He wanted a system in which the ruler would "cut off the hand of his own son if he steals, and would flog and stone his near relative if he fornicates."

Khomeini called for an entirely new regime, best described as clerical fascism:

> If a just mullah is placed in charge of the enforcement of canonical punishments . . . would he enforce them otherwise than how they were enforced in the days of the Prophet? . . . Would the Prophet have imposed less than a hundred lashes on the fornicator not previously chaste? Can the mullah reduce the amount of this punishment, thereby creating a divergence between his practice and that of the Prophet? Certainly not! The ruler . . . is no more than the executor of God's command and decree.

The rule of the "just mullah" (unsurprisingly, soon revealed to be Khomeini himself) would be a dictatorship based on sharia, Islamic law, ruthlessly enforced by religious tribunals, whose verdicts were absolute, not subject to appeal (how could anyone appeal a decision authorized by "the executor of God's command and decree"?). Those courts provided a legalistic veil that covered the thousands of arbitrary executions in the first months after the seizure of power.

There was never any ambiguity in Khomeini's words. Shortly after the seizure of power, Khomeini gave full vent to his rage against the West, promising that the Islamic Revolution—led by himself—would destroy its opponents in a global jihad.

> The great prophet of Islam carried in one hand the Koran and in the other a sword; the sword for crushing the traitors

> and the Koran for guidance. For those who could be guided, the Koran was their means of guidance, while for those who could not . . . the sword descended on their heads. . . . Islam is a religion of blood for the infidels but a religion of guidance for other people.[39]

In his dark vision of the future, Khomeini singled out the Jews (especially the Jewish state, Israel) and the Americans as his prime enemies. As for Israel, "the Koran bars its way—it must be removed." And Khomeini made it clear that he was talking about the Jews, not just Israel. There had been a close working relationship between the shah's Iran and Israel, which infuriated Khomeini, prompting him to ask, "Is the shah a Jew?"

But Israel was not an independent actor in Khomeini's view; behind the Israelis lurked the Great American Satan. "It is America which supports Israel and its well-wishers," he intoned. "It is America which considers Islam and the glorious Koran a source of harm to itself and wishes to remove both from its path."

Three American journalists—Judith Miller at *The New York Times*, Stephen Rosenfeld at *The Washington Post*, and I in an op-ed at *The Wall Street Journal*—obtained translations of long portions of the Khomeini diatribes, and published them. To our surprise, we then discovered that it was virtually impossible to find anyone in the policy or intelligence communities who was familiar with Khomeini's published doctrines, and we were subjected to heated criticism from government and academic experts who either denied the existence of the books, or denied that they said what we had reported. The low point of the moment (just prior to the shah's overthrow) came when Senator Henry Jackson held hearings on Khomeini. The CIA experts told him they did not believe the books were authentic, and suspected they were Israeli forgeries.

It's hard to imagine what they based this opinion on, since

they didn't have the texts. Rosenfeld got a phone call at the *Post* from the CIA, asking if they could borrow a copy of one of the books, since they didn't have it over in Langley. Officials at the American embassy in Tehran cabled the State Department in the early autumn (just a few months before Khomeini's revolution) to ask for some of the material—they, too, were without it. State was unable to provide it. Nonetheless, the State Department's Iran desk officer, Henry Precht, took advantage of a talk to a Foreign Service "Open Forum" to accuse Rosenfeld of peddling disinformation. Precht said that the books were either an unreliable collection of students' notes or an outright forgery. He would eventually be humiliated by the mullahs; just a couple of weeks after he traveled to Tehran to attempt to improve relations, the American embassy was overrun, and our diplomats taken hostage.

Nor was it at all credible to believe, as did most of the American experts and policy makers, that Khomeini had no political ambitions, or even if he did, that they would not extend beyond the domestic scene in Iran. In fact, Khomeini had developed quite an elaborate network with leading Arab terrorists, and, like other jihadis, he had benefitted from the support of the Soviet Union, especially their clandestine Farsi-language radio station, the National Voice of Iran. Moreover, in a move that demonstrated he was willing to cooperate with anyone, even infidels, in the struggle against the shah, Khomeini approved close working relations with the Iranian communist party, Tudeh. The communists gave him full support—unthinkable without Soviet approval—only to be violently smashed in 1983, once Khomeini had consolidated his rule.

Khomeini's flexibility was extremely broad based and long lasting, and should have demonstrated that one of the commonplaces about the Islamic world was false. Generations of Middle East experts maintained that there was an unbridgeable ideological chasm between Sunnis and Shiites (which includes the Iranians), but Khomeini and his successor, Ali Khamenei, claimed leadership of *all* Islam, and they supported—and were aided by—all manner of Sunni groups, above all the jihadis engaged in terrorism.

The Sunni/Shiite matter had an amusing echo early in the next century. The chairman of the Intelligence Committee in the U.S. House of Representatives, Silvestre Reyes of Texas, was asked the difference between Sunnis and Shiites, and he didn't know the answer. The difference boils down to a historical disagreement about the proper line of succession to the Prophet Mohammed. Sunnis and Shiites have been arguing about that ever since the Middle Ages, and it has played itself out into a very interesting disagreement over the relationship between mosque and state. In short, Sunnis have long believed that it is okay for religious leaders to function in government, since Mohammed's successors are known and with us, whereas Shiites have traditionally believed that the rightful successor to Mohammed has yet to come (or return, since he—the so-called Twelfth Imam—took refuge from his would-be assassins in the ninth century, and is still at the bottom of a well in Iran), and that therefore no religious leader is entitled to sit in a position of secular power. This is why the Ayatollah Sistani, who is the highest ranking and the most esteemed Shiite figure in Iraq, does not sit in the Iraqi parliament. He and other Iraqi Shiite clergy express their opinions about religious, political, and moral issues, but they don't sit in positions of political power.

This Shiite view of the proper relationship between religion and politics broke down in Iran with the revolution of 1979. When the Ayatollah Khomeini took over in that revolution, he said that not only was it allowable for religious people to govern civil society, but indeed it was now mandatory. Khomeini's most revealing line, spoken on the airplane from France to Iran when he was about to seize power, came in answer to the question of what his rule would mean for Iran. Khomeini said, in effect, that he didn't give a damn about Iran. He was leading all of Islam, not Iran, he said, and he would happily sacrifice everyone in Iran if he could accomplish the global triumph of Islam.

So Sunnis and Shiites traditionally have a historical and theological disagreement, but it isn't an unbridgeable chasm, as Khomeini's example shows. And in the history of the Iranian revolution, Sunnis and Shiites have worked mostly together from the very beginning—indeed, they worked together even before that revolution began. Iran's Revolutionary Guard Corps was created in the early 1970s in the Bekáa Valley of Lebanon, and was trained by Yasser Arafat's Fatah. Arafat was a super-Sunni who came out of the Muslim Brotherhood. In other words, today's most hardcore armed Shiite organization was trained by hardcore Sunnis. Sunnis and Shiites worked hand-in-glove to create a terrorist alliance that overthrew the shah and took power in Iran, and they have worked together ever since.

Those who argued that Khomeini had no interest in international action had to deny a large body of information that demonstrated the contrary. Khomeini received money, intelligence, and arms from the Syrian dictator Hafez al-Assad, a relationship that led to the Iranian-Syrian strategic alliance after the revolution, and continues today with Khomeini's successor and Assad's son, Bashar. For years, Khomeini worked closely with Yasser Arafat's Palestinian Liberation Organization (which was Sunni); Khomeini's praetorian guard, the Islamic Revolutionary Guards Corps, was trained by PLO guerrillas in Lebanon, beginning in the early 1970s. When Khomeini returned to Tehran, Arafat was his first official foreign guest (and the only foreign dignitary at the celebration of the first anniversary of the revolution), and the ayatollah promised a rich reward for services rendered: a royalty on every barrel of Iranian oil.

Khomeini even worked closely with atheists, such as the Marxists in the Popular Front for the Liberation of Palestine. So much for the comforting belief that he was simply a man of the cloth, a spiritual leader who would soon retire to his Koranic studies. He was true to his words: Ever since 1979, Iran has sponsored insurrectionary groups throughout the Muslim world, the Iranian version of the "export of the revolution." Hezbollah is the classic example: an international terror organization with a political base in Lebanon, aiming at the creation of an Iranian-style Islamic republic.

Despite all the evidence, it was hard to find anyone who recognized Khomeini for what he was, or who was even willing to take seriously the ayatollah's own words.

The failure to comprehend what Khomeini was all about contributed mightily to the American debacle in Iran, and to the subsequent failure of American policy, for the policy makers—from Carter down—did not take seriously the possibility that Khomeini might be worse than the shah. He was worse for the Iranian people, and, by orders of magnitude, worse for the United States. Not only did the Carter administration refuse to see Khomeini plainly, but it strove mightily to strengthen the new Iranian regime militarily.

Khomeini's fundamentalism did not exclude the acquisition of modern weapons, and postrevolutionary Iran had a hearty appetite for advanced American military technology. No sooner had the ayatollah returned to Tehran than the country's new military leaders bartered eagerly with Washington for a variety of products, above all spare parts for artillery and transport vehicles, and of course the air force, which was composed mostly of American fighter planes and helicopter warships. The Carter administration's representatives in Tehran and Washington were happy to comply, with one caveat: Everything had to be promptly paid for.

This technical problem had the ironic consequence of empowering the most fanatical elements of Khomeini's original coalition. The Iranians' first attempts to buy American weapons were sabotaged by their own fanatics, just as they had been in the final days of the shah. Radicals working at the Central Bank of the Islamic Republic of Iran blocked payment of all checks made out to any American entity.

This glitch would have provided a credible excuse for the Carter administration to rethink its desire to normalize relations with a man who had declared himself an enemy of the United States, but the Americans were so eager to consummate the sales—which the State Department and Pentagon viewed as a way to build good will between the two countries—that they resorted to all manner of acrobatic proposals. American citizens had fled Iran, leaving behind many of their personal effects. The administration came up with a clever scheme: The Iranian regime was hired to fly these things to the United States. A credit was then temporarily issued to Iran for services rendered, and then recycled back to the American government for the purchase of weapons, which were then loaded onto the same transport planes that had carried the Americans' property.

It was clever, to be sure, but it was too small to sate the Iranians' appetite. They were planning a major military campaign against the Kurds, and wanted lots of lethal equipment. A Pentagon team was duly dispatched to Tehran, and it soon informed Washington that the mullahs wanted to speed up the process. The White House was duly encouraged, and, dreaming of a diplomatic breakthrough that would normalize relations with the new regime, opened full-scale diplomatic negotiations.

In what was to become a great leitmotif of the next thirty years, American diplomats desperately worked for an agreement at all costs. One of the participants in the first meeting bragged that the "U.S. side was extraordinarily patient and understanding, repeatedly indicating willingness to review issues on their merits and to provide additional information where feasible."[40]

The Carter people were so encouraged that a couple of days later, Secretary of State Cyrus Vance met with Khomeini's personal adviser, Deputy Prime Minister for Revolutionary Affairs Ibrahim Yazdi, who brutally presented Iran's demands: The United States had to hand over the many Iranian "criminals" who had taken refuge in America; the United States must honor all the arms deals agreed with the shah; and Carter and his people had to remain silent about human rights, despite the mounting evidence of major bloodletting.

Instead of coming to grips with the unpleasant reality, the American diplomats strained to be understanding, invariably putting the most optimistic possible interpretation on the Iranians' behavior. Assistant Secretary of State Harold Newsom felt (as reported in the State Department cable describing the meeting) that

> . . . the Iranian suspicions of us were only natural in the post-revolutionary situation but that after a transition period common interests could provide a basis for future cooperation—"not on the scale of before but sufficient to demonstrate that Iran has not been 'lost' to us and to the West."

This upbeat report, with its insistence that the Iranians' "suspicions" were "only natural," instead of recognizing that Khomeini and his people hated the United States, was written barely a month before the American embassy in Tehran was seized. Up to the last, American military officials continued to negotiate the sale of spare parts for the Iranians to use against the Kurds.

The appeasement of the mullahs continued to the bitter end. After the embassy was seized, Carter approved a series of humiliating concessions in order to get the hostages back. The day before he left office, the president signed a series of executive orders to implement his concessions to the mullahs, of which one has long stuck in the craws of the returned hostages. According to Executive Order 12283, nobody subject to American law can sue the Islamic Republic for the destruction of the Tehran embassy or for the seizure, beating, and psychological torture of the American diplomats.

A FOOTNOTE: IRAN IN IRAQ DURING OPERATION IRAQI FREEDOM

The failure or refusal to see the true nature of the Iranian regime has continued to the present. Just as Carter's Iran experts had either failed, or willfully refused, to see the true nature of Khomeini, George W. Bush's Iran experts blocked the president from seeing information that showed Iranians were killing Americans in Iraq. As Bob Woodward tells us in *State of Denial,*[41] American officials acted to prevent the president from hearing about Iranian acts of war in Iraq, shortly after American forces overthrew Saddam Hussein:

> Some evidence indicated that the Iranian-backed terrorist group Hezbollah was training insurgents to build and use the shaped IEDs, at the urging of the Iranian Revolutionary Guard Corps. That kind of action was arguably an act of war by Iran against the United States. If we start putting

out everything we know about these things . . . the administration might well start a fire it couldn't put out.

Sixty pages later, he repeats the story:

The radical Revolutionary Guards Corps had asked Hezbollah, the terrorist organization, to conduct some of the training of Iraqis to use the EFPs, according to U.S. intelligence.

If all this were put out publicly, it might start a fire that no one could put out. . . . Second, if it were true, it meant that Iranians were killing American soldiers—an act of war.

So, it seems, the president wasn't told.

2

NONE SO BLIND AS THEY WHO WILL NOT SEE

His face is turned towards the past. Where we perceive a chain of events, he sees one single catastrophe which keeps piling wreckage upon wreckage and hurls it in front of his feet. The angel would like to stay, awaken the dead, and make whole what has been smashed. But a storm is blowing from Paradise; it has got caught in his wings with such violence that the angel can no longer close them. This storm irresistibly propels him into the future to which his back is turned, while the pile of debris before him grows skyward. This storm is what we call progress.

—Walter Benjamin

The huge literature on the Holocaust, and on Stalin's mass murders a decade earlier, has largely revolved around a question and a slogan. The question is, "How could it have happened?" The slogan is, "Never again." They are tied together by the assumption that if we can answer the question, we can ensure that such a thing will never happen again.

The easy and obvious answer to the "how?" question is that millions of people wanted it to happen, and they supported it with great passion and energy. Moreover, those millions of people cannot be easily written off as pagans or barbarians; they were Germans and Italians, and they were joined by Austrians and Belgians and Frenchmen and Swedes and Norwegians, along with Romanians, Poles, Hungarians, Czechs, Arabs, and others. The citizens of the most advanced cultures on earth enthusiastically engaged in unprecedented barbarism.

George Orwell got it just right when, in the winter of 1940, when Great Britain was under assault from Nazi bombers, he bitterly observed "highly civilized human beings are flying overhead, trying to kill me." He knew what his countrymen, and most of the intellectual elite of the West, had relegated to a quiet intellectual closet: Hitler and Mussolini had created monstrous mass movements in two of the most civilized, most cultured countries in Europe. The *Duce* and the Führer were wildly popular in the countries of Dante and Vivaldi, Beethoven and Goethe; they were not the products of some alien culture. They sprang from the most profound beliefs and passions of the highest cultures in the world, and the citizens of their countries loved them, supported them, and willingly fought and died for them. There was hardly any effective popular resistence in fascist Europe because most Italians and Germans supported the regimes, at least until things started to go badly (or, in the case of the Italians, until the world community turned against Mussolini after the invasion of Ethiopia).

We know all this. To be sure, there is always new information (especially from Soviet sources), but there is hardly a detail of the war, or the Holocaust, or the massacre of the kulaks in the Ukraine, or the purge trials, or the rise of Hitler and Mussolini, that has not been studied, often by brilliant scholars and philosophers. But have we understood them? Has this enormous effort by scholars, philosophers, novelists and poets, politicians and statesmen greatly improved our ability to recognize evil regimes and strengthened our resolve to confront them before they are able to threaten millions of innocents within their own borders and around the world? It appears not. There is not even a firm consensus about the causes of these evils, or even about the men who committed them.

In 1962–63, Hannah Arendt wrote five long articles for *The New Yorker*, which later became a widely debated book, *Eichmann in Jerusalem: A Report on the Banality of Evil*, in which she argued, among many controversial themes, that Eichmann was not a "moral monster," but a normal man without any particular animus for the Jews. He killed them, she said, because that was his job, not because he was driven to mass murder. "The trouble with Eichmann," she wrote, "was precisely that so many were like him, and that the many were neither perverted nor sadistic, that they were, and still are, terribly and terrifyingly normal." She even suggested that he had read Herzl, the founder of modern Zionism, and had then become a Zionist himself.

It was false; Eichmann was no Zionist. And if the extermination of millions of people can be defined as "normal," then the word has lost all meaning. Had Arendt argued that the case of Eichmann showed that men, even with the most sophisticated education in the most cultured countries, are capable of the most awful barbarisms, she would have been stating the obvious. It would then have been possible to move on to examine the circumstances under which such people become moral monsters, and to the broader question of why they attract such enthusiastic support. The obvious bears restating, because, as in the case of *Eichmann in Jerusalem*, and as in the behavior of so many of our leaders, it is often forgotten or ignored.

The debate over Arendt's thesis[1] has raged ever since, suggesting we are still far from the profound understanding we sought. If we cannot even agree whether mass murders are insane or normal, how can we possibly claim to have understood what happened?

Despite the extensive study of Hitler, despite the enormous literature on Stalin, Mussolini, Pol Pot, the Hutu Power leaders in Rwanda, and other horrors of our time, we seem still to suffer from Neville Chamberlain's failure: Our leaders and our intellectuals simply cannot imagine people so different from our image of human nature. Gourevitch had the same problem when he wrote his book about the Rwanda genocide, what he describes as "the peculiar necessity of imagining what is, in fact, real."[2]

That's the least of it. In the rare cases when leaders got it right, more often than not they were excoriated. The vilification of Winston Churchill in Great Britain by his political opponents in the years before Munich is well known. When Ronald Reagan delivered a speech on the Soviet Union, accurately describing it as an "evil empire," he was roundly denounced for being excessively provocative, as was George W. Bush when he spoke of an "axis of evil" following the terrorist attacks of 2001 in the United States. And in all three cases, members of the government and even professional civil servants blocked information from Churchill, Reagan, and Bush, or leaked contrary views in an attempt to undermine the leaders' credibility.

So we have to ask once again, why don't we see evil when it's right in front of our faces?

Our failure to understand the evil we faced (and face today) was not always merely of our own doing; it was often the result of successful deception by our enemies. Foreign leaders have figured out that democratic policy making is often driven by public opinion, and if they want a compliant administration in Washington, they can help it along by influencing Americans' views of the world. Many of the false images of evil enemies of the United States have been crafted by those enemies and skillfully placed in our media, or passed on by agents of influence. During the Reagan administration, the government tried to counter the Soviets' efforts to mislead the American people by publishing studies of Soviet "disinformation," which was a major undertaking of the KGB.

The Kremlin committed considerable intelligence resources all over the world to prevent the documentation of the truth about their activities. In the case of the Katyn massacre, for example, the Soviets conducted a "worldwide campaign to discredit and silence all those who knew about Katyn from personal experience, especially members of the International Medical Commission who lived . . . outside Beria's immediate sphere of influence."[3] Local Communists were enlisted in the campaign, as in Switzerland, where loyal comrades accused Professor Naville of being a Nazi collaborator, or in Italy, where Professor Palmieri at the University of Naples was put under surveillance by members of the Partito Comunista Italiano (PCI). He was subjected to open harrassment, even during his lectures, as a student of his later recounted:

> Suddenly and unexpectedly, one of our fellow students, a fellow known for his social communistic ideas, stands up. He shouts at the professor, threatens him, and yells for him to keep quiet. He says he is unworthy to teach, that he is a fascist, even a Nazi, and a liar who twists historical truth and blames the glorious Soviet soldiers . . . for the Katyn Massacre.[4]

Over the years, disinformation has become a large cottage industry in the United States, as actual agents, along with legitimate lobbyists and opportunistic or gullible journalists, spread soothing stories about hostile regimes. It isn't limited to bad guys: In the late 1930s and throughout the war, the British government had hundreds of agents of influence in the United States in order to counter traditional American isolationism, and the strong current of Yankee anti-British sentiment that fought Roosevelt's inclination to help the Brits whenever and however he could. That story revolves around the colorful character of William Stevenson, immortalized in *A Man Called Intrepid*,[5] who deployed other big personalities such as Roald Dahl.[6]

Most Americans do not know that Churchill was compelled to send some of his finest intelligence agents to the United States in order to combat profascist sentiment in the intellectual and political classes. But Churchill knew well that "America always does the right thing . . . after exhausting the alternatives," and Britain was facing destruction; he could not wait for us to exhaust all the available options. And if an ally had to fight for American public support, it was all the more urgent for our enemies to do so. During the Cold War, the Soviets mounted extensive PR campaigns to convince the American people of the Kremlin's benign intentions, and also to bring public pressure on the government to refrain from actions that would damage Soviet plans. Thus, the KGB supported campaigns against the deployment of missiles in Europe in the early 1980s, and was one of the principal sponsors of the "nuclear winter" campaign in favor of unilateral American nuclear disarmament.

There are other important reasons for our willful blindness, including partisan politics and ideology. Even without active Soviet involvement, the image of Stalin as a good friend and great man was advanced in good faith by Communists and their friends in keeping with the doctrine of "no enemies on the left." They did not tolerate any criticism of the Soviet Union, which was, in their view, the embodiment of the great socialist experiment. Thus the rejection of any suggestion that Stalin had inflicted death by famine on the Ukrainians. Thus the rejection of the view that the Soviet Union was morally monstrous, a rejection actively supported by *The New York Times*'s Walter Duranty, as noted in the first chapter. After the Second World War, the left-wing apologists for the Soviet Union were joined (at least until the outbreak of the Cold War) by those who cherished our wartime alliance with Stalin, and who were reluctant to admit that, having to fight a world war, we had fought alongside a monster.

The refusal to acknowledge the Nazi evil and try to do something to save the European Jews from annihilation was also due in part to another ideology, of an older and more malevolent sort: anti-Semitism. The WASP elite that governed the United States in the 1930s and 1940s was suspicious of (and often hostile to) foreigners, fought to keep immigration quotas small, and kept immigrant children out of many of the country's best schools and universities. This xenophobia was not restricted to Jews, but anti-Semitism was stronger than resentment of, say, Catholics in general, or Italians in particular. The Jews who had come to America in the early twentieth century seemed to the American establishment to be altogether too successful, and altogether too upwardly mobile. The statistics show what the old elite was worried about:

> The Russian Jews . . . arrived as families (about 40 percent of the Jewish immigrants were female, and 25 percent children); intended to stay (the average rate of repatriation from the United States was 7 percent for the Jews, 42 percent for everyone else); became fully urbanized; took almost no part in the competition for unskilled jobs; included an extraordinarily high proportion of entrepreneurs (in New York in 1914, every third immigrant); and [relied] . . . on cheap family labor, long hours, low profit margins, ethnic solidarity, vertical integration, and extremely high rates of standardization, specialization, and product differentiation. . . .
>
> By 1925, 50 percent of New York's Russian Jewish heads

> of households were in white-collar occupations, almost exclusively through entrepreneurship. As Andrew Bodly put it, "most Jewish immigrants . . . rose from the direst of poverty to positions of economic security and social respectability within fifty years when most of those around them did not."[7]

Just as they had in Western and Central Europe, the American Jews inverted the normal success story, according to which good education leads to economic success. The Jews took the reverse route: first making money, then educating the next generation. Thus the children of the first generation of immigrants went to college (and the generation after that became a major part of the professoriat). Already at the end of the First World War, some 20 percent of Harvard undergraduates were Jewish, and a few years later 80 to 90 percent of the student bodies at New York City College and Hunter College were Jews. With money and knowledge in hand, the Jews raced up the ladder of the American dream in short order: By 1925, more than half of Jewish immigrant businessmen had jobs that required formal education.

The combination of traditional stereotypes of Jews—greedy, pushy, clannish outsiders whose loyalty is always in doubt—with the considerable success of American Jews (most decidedly including the fact that the country's leading newspaper, *The New York Times*, was owned by Jews—the Sulzberger family) made for a toxic brew, as it had in Europe and Great Britain.

No surprise, then, that the State Department—staffed as it was with members of "good families" who had been educated at the best Ivy League colleges and universities—would fight against expanding the numbers of Jewish immigrants at the 1943 Bermuda Conference, or that they would not view the plight of the European Jews as warranting vigorous action by the United States, now facing a two-front global war.

Anti-Semitism worked hand-in-glove with the strategic decisions that the free peoples faced. It's difficult and painful for national leaders to call for harsh measures against even the most outspoken and obviously aggressive enemies. America was not inclined to fight the fascists until we had been directly attacked, nor were we engaged in serious antiterror actions prior to 9/11. Free societies rarely achieve durable consensus, and even a policy that begins with great popular support can lose it in a surprisingly short period of time, as George W. Bush learned at great cost when things got unexpectedly tough in Iraq. Knowing this, and recognizing that there is always a chance that any given strategy will fail, most leaders will shy away from confrontation. Politicians usually prefer prudence to valor, even when they see that there are potentially enormous costs to inaction.

Indifference, suspicion, or hatred of the Jews provides an escape from these tough decisions. One of the reasons the West was unwilling to send its armies to prevent the expansion of the Third Reich was that there was considerable sympathy for Hitler's crackdown on the German Jews, and Jewish refugees from the Nazi occupation were not welcome elsewhere. This went beyond the famous cases of British and American resistance to Jewish immigration, including the truly ghastly story of the MS *St. Louis*, which sailed across the Atlantic in 1939 with hundreds of German Jews, only to be denied entry to Cuba. They were forced to return to Europe (more than 80 percent of Americans polled by *Fortune* magazine approved). The Swiss government insisted that German Jews be identified with a red *J* in their passports, the better to keep them out.

The same considerations apply on the tactical level. Once the war was upon them, Western leaders were infamously unwilling to take action against the Nazi death camps, even though they were legitimate military targets. And when Roosevelt and Churchill, both of whom were sympathetic to the plight of

Hitler's victims, were asked to do something to save the European Jews, they faced determined opposition from their diplomats and military officials.

Today, our enemies exploit this indifference, suspicion, and hatred of the Jews to paralyze our response to their attacks on the West. The Iranians and their Islamist allies hate the Jews and wish to destroy them, while many in the West are all too willing to believe that there is some truth to the Islamists' claim that we have no legitimate reason to fight radical Islamic terrorism, and have been manipulated by Israel, or sinister Jewish (or "neoconservative") cabals within America and other free societies.

The case of the celebrated British-American historian Tony Judt is exemplary. Judt, who believes that Israel should cease to be a Jewish state, argues[8] that sensitivity to the Holocaust is a very recent, and a regrettable development. In the immediate postwar period, he claims, West Europeans "preferred to forget collaboration and other indignities and emphasize instead the heroic resistance movements, national uprisings, liberations, and martyrs." He concludes that "no one—not Germans, not Austrians, not French or Dutch or Belgians or Italians—wanted to recall the suffering of the Jews or the distinctive evil that had brought it about."

His prime literary example of the Europeans' desire to forget about the great evil of the Holocaust is Primo Levi, whose famous memoir about his experiences at Auschwitz, *Se questo è un uomo*, was originally turned down in 1946 by the prestigious publishing house Einaudi. Judt says,

> At that time, and for some years to come, it was Bergen-Belsen and Dachau, not Auschwitz, which stood for the horror of Nazism; the emphasis on political deportees rather than racial ones conformed better to reassuring postwar ac-

> counts of wartime national resistance. Levi's book was eventually published, but in just 2,500 copies by a small local press. Hardly anyone bought it; many copies of the book were remaindered in a warehouse in Florence and destroyed in the great flood there in 1966.

Judt is substantially wrong about the literary history, as about the "desire to forget." Levi's book was indeed turned down by Einaudi, and originally published in 1947 by the obscure De Silva publishing house in Turin. But just eleven years later, in 1958, Einaudi did publish it, and by 1968 it had gone through twelve Italian editions, as well as French, German, British, American, Dutch, and Finnish translations. Giorgio Bassani's *Il giardino dei Finzi-Contini,* another international bestseller, told the story of an Italian Jewish family in Ferrara during fascism, and its destruction by the Nazis. It was published in 1962, and the Academy Award–winning film was on the screen in 1971.

Moreover, by the very early 1960s, there was quite a considerable Holocaust literature; Hannah Arendt's *Eichmann in Jerusalem*, which kicked off a worldwide debate, appeared in 1963, and Raul Hilberg's *The Destruction of the European Jews* (which, like Levi's masterpiece, was published only after years of great difficulty) appeared from Quadrangle in 1961, and became a classic. And whereas Judt claims that nobody in Europe wanted to hear about the distinctive evil that had brought about the slaughter of the Jews, Karl Dietrich Bracher's work on the collapse of the Weimar Republic came out in 1955, and his book on the National Socialist seizure of power—which discusses Nazi anti-Semitism at considerable length—was published a mere five years later, and provided the basis for an exhaustive television series in West Germany that had considerable effect.

Judt writes as if Primo Levi's book were an exemplar of Holocaust literature, but Levi was arrested because he was a partisan, not as a Jew. His Jewishness was important once he entered the concentration camp system, but it is hardly a central theme of his book. His concern is with the destruction of the humanity of men; his is a universal message, not one limited to Jews. As Levi puts it near the end of the book:

> It's difficult to destroy man, almost as to create him: it wasn't easy, it wasn't short, but you Germans succeeded. Here we stand, docile under your glares: you have nothing more to fear from us: not acts of revolt, not challenging words, not even a judgmental look.[9]

It's not just, or even primarily, about Jews; it's about evil. And when Judt complains that overattention to the Holocaust—and from there to a moral justification of Israel—has obscured the universal problem of evil, it's a perverse position indeed. It's hard to see how our understanding of evil can be advanced by spending *less* time studying the Holocaust.

Judt thinks the focus on the Holocaust has been overdone, and passionate anti-Zionist that he is, he dislikes its intimate linkage to Israel.

> My fear is that two things have happened. By emphasizing the historical uniqueness of the Holocaust while at the same time invoking it constantly with reference to contemporary affairs, we have confused young people. And by shouting "anti-Semitism" every time someone attacks Israel or defends the Palestinians, we are breeding cynics. For the truth is that Israel today is not in existential danger. And Jews today here in the West face no threats or prejudices remotely comparable to those of the past—or comparable to contemporary prejudices against other minorities.

He asks, rhetorically, if Jews anywhere in the West don't justifiably feel safer than "illegal immigrants" (his quotation marks) in the United States, or blacks in Switzerland, or Romanians in Italy. (He thinks the answer is obvious—the Jews feel more comfortable than the others—but the mounting tempo of Jewish emigration from France and Great Britain suggests otherwise.) And that leads him to his real point: "We have attached the memory of the Holocaust so firmly to the defense of a single country—Israel—that we are in danger of provincializing its moral significance."

Only someone bound and determined to single out Israel for moral censure could argue with a straight face that serious study of the Holocaust is anything other than an analysis of evil. In his efforts to condemn Israel and advance the Palestinian cause, Judt caricatures Israel by claiming it faces no existential threat (it is hard to find any reference to Iran in his analysis), and excuses the fanaticism of its enemies while sternly condemning any and all Israeli excesses.

Finally, our willful blindness to evil is caused in part by the traditional, optimistic American view of human nature, combined with the spectacular series of events in the last quarter of the twentieth century that I have called "the Second Democratic Revolution."[10] In those years, dictators fell all over the world, from Europe and Asia to Latin America and even Africa. Tyrants were sent into exile, and former political prisoners led new, freely elected governments based on the people's right to choose their system of government and the men and women who should administer it. The cult of the state was challenged almost everywhere, and it seemed that a political millenium was at hand.

The spectacular success of democracy reinforced the happy thought that the world had fundamentally changed, that war was a thing of the past, and that violence among men was on the decline. It seems preposterous that anyone could believe the happy thought, after the bloodiest century in human history. Even if we hadn't gone through two world wars and added the word "genocide" to the dictionary, centuries of human experience should have put the lie to such unbridled optimism.

Contrary to the declarations of "the end of history" and the arrival of a universal era of good feelings, such a transformation of human nature was extremely unlikely, and in any case it wasn't going to happen without extraordinary leadership. Those who embraced the myth of a happy new world order simply ignored the history of democratic revolutions. No country in the past had moved from dictatorship to democracy without considerable violence. The first wave of democratic revolution—the last quarter of the eighteenth century—saw every Western country undergo some political spasm aimed against the traditional monarchies. The two biggest events were the American and French Revolutions.

This was the watershed of the modern world—the first modern world war. Until the mid-1970s it was widely taken for granted that the arrival of democracy was always accompanied by violent revolution, perhaps accompanied by civil war, and quite possibly war between nations on a vast scale. Just a bit more than a generation ago, as Spain's military dictator Generalissimo Franco lay dying in Madrid, it was next to impossible to find any knowledgeable person who believed that Spain could become a democratic country without a replay of the bloody civil war of the 1930s. Spaniards themselves were thoroughly convinced that they would do just that. "We kill the bulls, after all," they liked to say; they were a violent people, and the old order would not go quietly into the dark night of fallen autocracies.

And yet Spain accomplished a seemingly miraculous democratic revolution, paradoxically organized and managed by icons of the old order: King Juan Carlos I and a now-forgotten

Franco loyalist, Adolfo Suárez, along with a talented leader of the socialist opposition, Felipe González. Portugal followed suit shortly thereafter, albeit with some dramatic moments and a few street clashes.

The smooth transition in Spain and Portugal ushered in the Age of the Second Democratic Revolution, the years of Reagan, Thatcher, John Paul II, Havel, Walesa, Sharansky, and Bukovsky, replete with revolutions from Chile to Taiwan, from Romania and the rest of the Soviet empire to South Africa and Zambia. With the indifference to history so characteristic of our world, we quickly forgot the old conventional wisdom. We soon took it for granted that neither war nor violence is required to end tyranny. All we need is patience and the proper invocation of the new rules: free and fair elections, the rule of law, and so forth. History had ended, liberal democracy was triumphant.

In the Clinton years, for example, it was widely believed that all future conflict would be solely economic. The age of military warfare had passed, henceforth products, markets, and human ingenuity would determine who is rightly top dog and who needs to get with the program. In keeping with the new vision, the defense budget was slashed, military men and women were treated with contempt by the president and his wife, and we turned inward. After all, if historical inevitability ruled, why bother with national security? Tyranny was considered a passing phenomenon, headed for the ash heap, and certainly no threat to us.

The belief in the inevitability of peace and democracy rested on one of the great conceits of the European Enlightenment, namely the belief in the perfectibility of man. In this view, man's basic goodness (as found in "the state of nature") had been corrupted by a selfish society (a notion that finds much favor among today's more extreme Greens), but that once the heavy weight of misguided ideas was lifted, man's intrinsic goodness would reemerge. In our modern rendition of that Enlightenment folly, a patient appeal to reason, accompanied by unlimited good will, should be sufficient to change the world.

In the face of centuries of violent human history that indicate precisely the opposite, Americans are the first people in the history of the world to believe that peace is the normal condition of mankind, or at least that it can become our normal state. This quaint article of faith blends nicely with two other American conceits, that all people are equally good, and all problems can be solved, if only one has enough patience and good will.

Yet ever since ancient times, the finest strategic thinkers have insisted that strength, and the willingness to use it, is the surest path to peace. And with rare exceptions, "peace" invariably describes the conditions that are imposed by the victors on their enemies after a war. War, and preparation for war, are the normal conditions of mankind, while peace is extremely rare. Most conflicts are not "resolved" through negotiation; they are settled on the battlefield.

In addition to the confusion about human nature, and the consequent tendency to misread recent events, in recent years, the doctrines of political correctness and multiculturalism have added another theme: the notion that all cultures and practices are entitled to the same respect. This makes it harder than ever to identify evil regimes.

It's not easy for modern intellectuals to accept the true nature of the regimes that followed the fascist and communist revolutions because of the long-discredited but still popular theory that revolutions are always a good thing, and are invariably a righteous popular eruption against social and economic misery inflicted by greedy oppressive governments. In that view, revolutions are signs of progress, another step along the road to modernity. But, especially in the twentieth century, many important revolutions were reactionary outbursts *against* modernity, a desperate attempt to restore an earlier (and often imaginary) style of politics in which the state, or the leader, made most of the fundamental decisions, thereby sparing citizens the many agonizing choices that afflict modern man.

IRAN

The Islamic Revolution in Iran in 1979 was precisely that. When the Iranians overthrew the shah thirty years ago, it was fashionable in the West to hail the revolution and to "explain" it as an explosion of freedom against a tyrannical dictator. But it was the opposite; Khomeini's attack on the shah was not that the shah was insufficiently modern and liberal, but rather too modern, too tolerant, too progressive. Khomeini promised to turn back the clock, not advance it; there would be less freedom for women and for infidels, and medieval methods of "justice," like stoning to death, would be reinstated. Khomeini offered the Iranians a chance to allay their terrible fear of freedom.

To be sure, many of Khomeini's supporters deluded themselves into believing that his promises were just rhetoric. Others hoped that once in power, he would "moderate." But he didn't. He plunged Iran into a new Dark Ages, just as Hitler plunged Germany back into a (largely imaginary) ancient mindset with pseudoscientific concepts of race replacing the older tribal categories. Both were "revolutionary" leaders of a peculiar modern sort: contemporary political techniques merged with archaic ideas.

The lack of understanding of the Iranian regime is so great that even a deputy secretary of state, Richard Armitage, could say in the first years of the George W. Bush administration, "Iran is some kind of democracy."

In other words, the great enterprise to understand "how could it have happened?" has failed. We have the facts, but we're unwilling to admit their meaning, and act on it, which is why "never again" is an empty phrase, rendered thus by the daily events of our world.

Natan Sharansky tells us that the basic lesson of his lifelong campaign for freedom is that for the oppressed in tyrannical countries, the primary challenge is finding the inner strength to confront evil; for those of us who live in free countries, the primary challenge is finding the moral clarity to see evil.[11] We have a hard time reaching and sustaining that moral clarity.

Just as the West insisted that we could deal peacefully with Hitler, just as we reassured ourselves that Stalin was a decent man and Soviet dictators were just like anybody else, so today our leaders refuse to recognize that other evil regimes are on the march. The clearest example is Iran, where an evil regime oppresses its people and wages war against us.

The simple facts regarding Iran are readily available, and extremely easy to understand. We are dealing with a radical Islamist regime that came to power in 1979, when the Iranian revolution overthrew the shah. Immediately thereafter, it declared war against the United States, branding us the Great Satan. The Iranians have been at war against us for thirty years, and prior to 9/11 the Iranian regime was directly or indirectly responsible for the murder of more Americans than any other country or organization in the world. In its annual review of international terrorism, the State Department routinely names Iran as the world's leading terror sponsor, and for good reason. Iran created the Islamic Jihad Organization, along with Hezbollah, arguably the most dangerous terror group. And Iran long supported al Qaeda, as is demonstrated by one of the most oft-forgotten documents in contemporary American history. In the fall of 1998, the American government indicted Osama bin Laden and al Qaeda. There is a paragraph in the indictment that reads as follows:

> Al Qaeda forged alliances with the National Islamic Front in the Sudan and with the government of Iran and its associated terrorist group, Hezbollah, for the purpose of working together against their perceived common enemies in the West, particularly the United States.

The American government knew that Iran was working hand-in-glove with anti-American terrorists, both internationally and within the United States itself, where the Iranians had supported the first World Trade Center bombing, commanded by the "blind sheikh" Omar Abdel-Rahman. We knew, further, that the Iranians were working in cooperation with the Muslim Brotherhood, the Egyptian radical jihadist organization that was behind the assassination of Anwar Sadat, and had supported the Ayatollah Khomeini's overthrow of the shah of Iran.

No one should have been surprised when the Iranian regime supported the terror war against us in Afghanistan and Iraq, but in fact many tried to deny it. I had direct experience of the unwillingness of top American officials to believe the Iranians were attacking American forces in Afghanistan. In December 2001, I helped organize a meeting in Rome with some knowledgeable Iranians, at least one of whom ran considerable personal risk by coming to talk to us. We learned, in great detail, that the Iranians had sent assassins to Afghanistan to kill American soldiers. This information was passed on to American Special Forces, who verified it, and then took action against the would-be assassins. Nonetheless, both CIA and State Department officials (including Secretary of State Colin Powell and Director of Central

Intelligence George Tenet) were enraged when they learned of the meetings, and blocked further contacts with the sources who had provided the (accurate, and life-saving) information.

Like the high State Department official quoted by Bob Woodward who didn't want President Bush to learn about Iranian "acts of war" against our troops in Iraq, Tenet and Powell apparently did not want to face the fact that Iran was trying to defeat us. But over the next several years, it became impossible to deny, as a few typical news stories show.

In Afghanistan

- In the summer of 2007, former White House counterterrorism official Richard Clarke, referring to the discovery of heavy arms, C-4 explosives, and advanced roadside bombs to the Taliban for use against NATO forces, stated flatly, "It is inconceivable that it is anyone other than the Iranian government that's doing it."[12]
- At the same time, Undersecretary of State Nicholas Burns announced on CNN that "There's irrefutable evidence the Iranians are now doing this, it's certainly coming from the government of Iran. It's coming from the Iranian Revolutionary Guard Corps command, which is a basic unit of the Iranian government."[13]
- This was confirmed by the top American army officer in Afghanistan. "The top NATO commander in Afghanistan alleged Thursday that the Iranian military was involved in a shipment of sophisticated explosive devices intercepted by his troops in western Afghanistan last month."
- "U.S. Army General Dan McNeill, the commander of NATO's 40,000-strong International Security Assistance Force, said the convoy intercepted on Sept. 5 contained 'a number of ad-

vanced technology improvised explosive devices.' 'This weapons convoy clearly, geographically, originated in Iran,' McNeill told reporters in Kabul. 'It is difficult for me to conceive that this convoy could have originated in Iran and come to Afghanistan, without at least the knowledge of the Iranian military,' he said. . . ."[14] The British military said much the same thing: "This confirms our view that elements within Iran are supporting the Taliban," a spokesman for the British embassy in Kabul said. "We have previously raised the issue of arms to the Taliban with the Iranians and will continue to do so."[15]

- The following spring, Lieutenant General Carter Ham said ". . . the Iranian support of the Taliban has continued."[16]

In Iraq

There was abundant evidence of Iranian support to various elements of the insurgency, both Sunni and Shiite. Major General William Caldwell, for example, said "It's not all Sunni insurgents but . . . we do know that there is a direct awareness by Iranian intelligence officials that they are providing support to some select Sunni insurgent elements." And Major General Rick Lynch said the evidence suggested some degree of Iranian influence among Sunni as well as Shiite extremists.[17]

General David Petraeus noted that the Iranians were "funding, over the last several years, certainly hundreds of millions of dollars of assistance to different Shi'a militia groups, and we have found evidence very recently of assistance being provided to Sunni Arab groups as well. One of the Sunni insurgent leaders was just over in Tehran."[18]

Major General Michael Barbero, deputy director for regional operations in the U.S. Joint Chiefs of Staff, pointed out that we had obtained first-hand information about Iranian support for terrorists in Iraq:

> "Detainees in American custody have indicated that Iranian intelligence operatives have given support to Sunni insurgents, and then we've discovered some munitions in Baghdad neighborhoods which are largely Sunni that were manufactured in Iran."[19]

General Caldwell added a further wrinkle, namely that Iraqi Shiite terrorists were actually being trained in Iran itself.

> "We have, in fact, found some cases recently where Iranian intelligence services have provided to some Sunni insurgent groups some support," Caldwell told reporters, adding that he was aware of only Shiite extremists being trained inside Iran. Caldwell cited a collection of munitions on a nearby table that he said were made in Iran and found two days ago in a majority-Sunni neighborhood in Baghdad.[20]

If any doubt remained, the American military repeatedly announced the arrest of Iranian and Lebanese Hezbollah military officers in Iraq, where they were engaged in arming, training, and overseeing Iraqi and foreign terrorists. In late October 2008, for example, Iraq police and border guards arrested seven members of the Iranian Revolutionary Guards Corps inside Iraq. "The seven Iranians were likely members of Qods Force, the elite special operations branch [that] reports directly to Ayatollah Ali Khamenei, Iran's supreme leader."[21]

At about the same time, *The New York Times* reported on a batch of declassified intelligence documents that documented "in detail an elaborate network used by Iraqis to gain entry into Iran and train under Iranian supervision."[22] The movements of the Iraqi trainees were often scheduled to coincide with religious pilgrimages between the two countries, when millions of the faithful traveled back and forth. They stayed in an elaborate network of safe houses in both countries.

Elsewhere in the region, a captured letter revealed that Osama's son, Saad bin Laden, was a key intermediary between al Qaeda and the Iranian regime.[23] Saad bin Laden, who had been in Iran ever since al Qaeda was driven out of Afghanistan in 2001, was the intended recipient of the letter, written by Ayman al-Zawahiri (al Qaeda's number two) to the Iranian Revolutionary Guards Corps. Zawahiri thanked the IRGC for its "monetary and infrastructure assistance," without which it would not have been possible for al Qaeda to carry out ten terrorist attacks in Yemen in the previous ten months.

Further evidence of Iranian support for terrorism throughout the region was presented in early 2009 by the Saudis,[24] who publicly released a list of eighty-five "most wanted" terrorists, eighty-three of whom were Saudis, and forty-one of whom were said to be "last seen in Iran, or in the Iranian-Afghan-Pakistani triangle." One of them, Abdullah al-Qarawi, was described as a Saudi in charge of al Qaeda's operations in the Persian Gulf and recruited jihadis for terrorist attacks in Afghanistan, and was said to have more than a hundred other Saudis under his guidance in Iran, "where they move about freely." He had been working out of Iran for three years.

It required a strong will in order to deny the reality of Iran's war against us, but there were some who found the necessary resolve. Unfortunately for their case, the Iranians themselves admitted it to a British diplomat as early as 2005. According to a BBC documentary,[25] by that time Coalition forces in Iraq had proof that the Iranians were manufacturing the lethal IEDs that were the greatest single source of casualties to our men and women there. The proof was delivered to the Iranians, along with a stern message from President Bush that warned we would consider this an act of war and act accordingly.

The Iranians reacted by approaching the British UN Ambassador in London, and offering a deal: They would stop killing our troops in Iraq if we would stop trying to end the Iranian nuclear project.

The deal was rejected.

At the same time, the Iranian regime was waging an equally ferocious war against its own citizens.

THE WAR AGAINST THE IRANIAN PEOPLE

In Andrei Sakharov's invaluable formulation, if you want to know how a country will behave internationally, look at the way it treats its own people. Iran is at once the world's leading supporter of terrorism and one of the cruelest oppressors of its own people. As Sakharov said, the mullahs treat their own people the same way they would like to treat the rest of the world.

Iran's designated external enemies are primarily the Jews (sometimes referred to as "Zionists"), the Israelis, and the Americans, the lesser and greater Satans. The internal enemies comprise anyone who challenges the wisdom or legitimacy of the regime, especially if he is a representative of a large and potentially powerful group: ethnic and religious minorities and, above all, women, who are viewed as the ultimate source of corruption. Khomeini was a supreme misogynist, and the laws of the Islamic Republic single out women for special horrors and humiliation.

Iran's maltreatment of women puts it in highly restricted company. Only two countries executed women in 2007: Iran and Saudi Arabia. (China has already joined the other two this year.)

The oppression, torture, and execution of Iranian women,

sometimes by stoning, have the full force of the laws of the Islamic Republic. A woman's worth is officially defined as half of a man's. Iranian law provides for the payment of "blood money" in the case of violent crime or accident, and harm to a man costs twice as much as the same damage to a woman. A man killed in an automobile incident gets twice as much as a woman killed in the same event. Incredibly, if a pregnant woman is killed, the guilty party pays the full assessment for the dead male fetus but only half as much for its mother.

Misogyny is particularly cruel when it comes to the barbaric practice of stoning. Both men and women can be stoned to death, but men have some chance of survival. The men are only buried in the ground up to their waist, and (unless they have been sentenced for a capital offense) if they can claw their way out of the earth before they are killed, their lives are spared. In early 2009, three stoning sentences were enforced on men, and one of them survived. Not so with women, who are buried up to their shoulders. They have no hope of freeing their hands and arms. Their doom is certain.[26]

Women are systematically dominated by men in every aspect of civil life. No Iranian woman, no matter how old or distinguished, can marry without her father's or paternal grandfather's consent, or if that cannot be obtained, the approval of a religious tribunal. Mothers don't count. Indeed, although a woman is only recognized as a citizen once she is a mother (and therefore has no legal standing so long as she is single), mothers have no say in the marriage of their children. It is all in the hands of the men.

Given this absolute authority, there are many cases in which very young girls (the legal age for marriage is thirteen) are married off to older, even elderly, men because of financial advantage. This sort of treatment also takes place at the opposite end of the timeline: Girls are instructed to marry very young boys (who are eligible at fifteen). Unsurprisingly, a very high percentage of divorces involve partners who married when they were under nineteen years of age.

Men can divorce their wives whenever they wish, but women must prove that the husband has misbehaved, including drug addiction, conviction for crimes, or failure to provide for her subsistence. Since the men are invariably favored by the courts, women often find it impossible to get a divorce without the husband's cooperation, and this generally requires them to formally renounce their legal right to financial support. A recent study in Qom concluded that more than 90 percent of divorced women had either abandoned all claim to support, or had negotiated a reduction.

Almost all of the tiny handful of Iranian women in positions of authority (only 4 percent of the members of the last Parliament were female, and not one was a candidate for a leadership position) officially endorse the subordination of women.[27] One such parliamentarian, Nayereh Akhavan, remarked, in fine Khomeini-style rhetoric, "Man's right to divorce comes from the fact that because women are emotional, they may destroy everything. But with the right to divorce in man's hands, they will stop the destruction of the family." It is hard to imagine that any woman advocating gender equality in Iran could be elected to public office; the mullahs have complete control over the electoral lists. Even the celebrated Nobel Peace Prize winner Shirin Ebadi is subjected to death threats, along with her daughter. As Ebadi elegantly noted in an open letter to the chief of police in Tehran in April 2008, "I don't owe anyone and in my legal practice I represent victims of human rights abuse free of charge. Therefore, people who wish me dead are opposed not to me personally, but to my opinions and beliefs."

Ebadi was working on a number of high-profile political, ideological, and human rights cases, including the murder cases of two women, Zahra Kazemi and Zahra Bani Yaghoub. The regime slowly increased the pressure against her, culminating in December 2008, when her human rights center in Tehran was shut down, her documents were seized, her computers searched, and a mob demonstrated in front of her house.[28]

The same prejudicial treatment applies to guardianship of children. Iranian civil law denies women the right to legal guardianship; the father cannot even delegate parental authority to his wife. If he dies, control passes to his own father. And even if both are absent or dead, the child then becomes a ward of the state, never of the mother. Even married mothers cannot do any of the routine things they do in the West: They can't open a bank account in their children's name, can't approve medical treatment, can't buy a house for the children.

Women have no right to own property of their own, and a wife only receives a fraction of her husband's estate if she is widowed; and of course sons receive twice as much as daughters. If there is more than one wife, the same fraction of the estate—one-eighth or one-fourth, depending on whether there were children—is divided among the widows.

The most humiliating case is if there are no children, and the husband dies. The widow gets the usual one-fourth of the estate, and the rest goes to the state. As a leading Iranian feminist puts it, "The government is closer to that dead man than his wife with whom he has lived an entire lifetime."

Even citizenship is patrilineal. If an Iranian woman marries a foreigner, the children are not considered to be Iranian, unless the mother has received special approval from the Interior Ministry, and she may even lose her own citizenship.

Polygamy is fine for men (up to four "permanent" wives are permitted, plus a limitless number of "temporary" partners) but polyandry is denied to women. The chair of the Parliamentary Women's Faction endorses polygamy: "This is eventually in the interest of women and women should accept it." Consequently, men rarely if ever stand trial for adultery, while female adulterers can be stoned to death. Not surprisingly, most of the cases of women murdering their husbands stem from the man's infidelity, whatever the largesse of the "temporary marriage" proviso. Here again, the double standard is in full force. Women who murder their unfaithful husbands are punished, while a man will go scot-free for killing his wife if he discovers—or even imagines—that she has been intimate with other men.

Finally, just as the Jews were once forced to wear distinctive clothing, so Iranian women must wear the hijab. This applies to all women, whatever their religion. Muslims, Baha'is, Christians, and Jews all must dress in the same way.

No surprise, then, that when the mullahs discovered to their horror that many more women than men were pursuing higher education, laws were drafted to reduce the number of women admitted to university study, and to forbid travel for single women outside the Islamic Republic. No surprise, either, that Iranian activists are quietly circulating a petition calling for equal rights for women. Their objective is to gather a million signatures and then submit it to the parliament. The regime dreads this—it is hardly a secret, having appeared on many blogs, and announced in public meetings in the major cities—and anyone caught soliciting signatures goes straight to jail.

The brutal treatment of Iranian women by the mullahcracy is a daily occurrence, not an isolated case. On an official radio broadcast in early March 2005, a well-known analyst reported that "at least fifty-four Iranian girls and young women, between the ages of sixteen and twenty-five, are sold on the streets of Karachi in Pakistan on a daily basis." The analyst, Mahboubeh Moghadam, added that there were at least three hundred thousand runaway girls in Iran, the result, in Moghadam's words, of "the government policy which has resulted in poverty and the deprival of rights for the majority of people in society."

Professor Donna M. Hughes, at the University of Rhode Island, one of the few Western scholars reporting on these horrors, says that the enslaved women are typically sold to people in the Arab countries of the Persian Gulf, such as Qatar, Kuwait, and the United Arab Emirates. But the slave trade is not limited to the Islamic world. Rings operating from Tehran have sold Iranian girls in France, Britain, and Turkey as well. There are countless examples of the maltreatment of Iranian women, but none so dramatic as the case of a foreigner of Iranian origin who tried to expose the regime's systematic oppression of those seeking greater freedom for all Iranians.

In the summer of 2003, a middle-aged Iranian-Canadian journalist named Zahra Kazemi was arrested in Tehran while taking photographs of hoodlums beating up young people demonstrating against the regime. A few days later she turned up dead in a local military hospital. The regime denied requests from the family and the Canadian government to examine the body, insisted that she had fallen in her prison cell and died of head injuries resulting from the fall, denied that anyone had beaten her, and hastily buried her without any proper autopsy.

The Kazemi family never believed the regime's story, but efforts to get at the truth were fruitless. It was one of those things that "everybody knew" but could not be documented sufficiently to convince the skeptics and apologists for the mullahs. Then, in the spring of 2005, a medical doctor named Shahram Azam was granted asylum in Canada, and presented a first-hand account of the terrible death of Zahra Kazemi.[29]

Dr. Azam said he examined Kazemi in a military hospital in Tehran on June 26, 2003. He said he found horrific injuries to her entire body that demonstrated torture and rape. By the time he examined her—an examination limited by the Islamic republic's sexist restrictions that made it illegal for a male doctor to look at her genital area—Kazemi was unconscious and her body was covered with bruises. According to Dr. Azam, she had a skull fracture, two broken fingers, missing fingernails, a crushed big toe, a smashed nose, deep scratches on her neck, and evidence of flogging on her legs and back.

"I could see this was caused by torture," Azam told Canadian journalists. He added that the nurse who examined Kazemi's genitals told him of "brutal damage." He believes she was tortured and raped.

All of this is consistent with what we have learned about the methods of torture routinely employed in Iranian prisons, as reported by leading international human rights organizations such as Human Rights Watch, Amnesty International, Reporters Without Borders, and the State Department's survey of human rights around the world. These sadistic practices are directed against all critics and opponents of the regime, but they are carried out with particular energy when the victim is female, even if she is world-famous.

In mid-December 2008, the human rights organization created by Nobel Prize–winner Shirin Ebadi (an organization paid for with her prize money) was closed down by Iranian security forces, who then sacked the place, carrying off documents and computers. On January 1, 2009, a rented crowd gathered in front of Ebadi's home, sprayed anti-American graffiti on the walls, and shouted threats at her and her family.

MINORITIES

Roughly half of Iranians are Persian; the others are members of various ethnic groups and tribes: Azeris, Kurds, Balouch, Ahwazi Arabs, Lurs, and so forth. A very small part of the population is non-Muslim, of which the Jews and the Baha'is are the best known, and the Zoroastrians are perhaps the largest. The mullahs view them all with hatred and suspicion, and the "minority" communities are constantly concerned about the security of their people. From time to time, ethnic cleansing campaigns are launched against them, lately with particular intensity against the Ahwazis, Zoroastrians, and Baloch. The campaign against the Kurds dates to the first months of the Islamic Republic, and has never stopped. Indeed, the mullahs not only attack Iranian Kurds, but participate in armed incursions and artillery attacks against the Kurds in northern Iraq.

In the south, the regime has been conducting a secret ethnic-cleansing campaign against the Ahwazi Arabs. British human rights activist Peter Tatchell calls it "a sustained, bloody campaign of intimidation and persecution against its Arab minority," waged in secret to the great indifference of most of the world. It's the usual pattern. Sixteen Ahwazis were sentenced to death on the basis of confessions produced under torture, and the executions "seem designed to silence protests by Iran's persecuted ethnic Arabs." The government has announced plans to transfer a million Arabs to another region of the country, recalling Stalin's efforts to solve his "nationalities problem" by similar means.

Anyone trying to dig out the facts of the court cases runs up against a hard stone wall. Foreign journalists are severely restricted, and local reporters are intimidated with threats of imprisonment. Even so, some elements of this remarkable repression have filtered out. For one thing, all Ahwazi trade unions, student groups, and political parties have been banned. In one year, starting from October 2005, no fewer than a quarter of a million Arabs were moved from their villages, and another four hundred thousand are facing similar prospects in the near future. Dozens of towns and villages have been bulldozed into the sand. At the same time, Persians are offered interest-free loans to move into new towns in the vacated areas, and plans call for half a million to arrive in the near future. All Arab newspapers and schoolbooks have been banned, and all instruction is in Farsi (a pattern repeated in all minority ethnic areas). Eighty percent of Ahwazi children suffer from malnutrition, even though they live in the potentially richest area of the country; 90 percent of the oil comes from there.

As Stalin did to the Soviet Union's "nationalities," the Iranian regime simply kicks out the locals, transferring ownership of the land to the Iranian Revolutionary Guards Corps' front organizations and other state-owned enterprises, thereby enriching the mighty. The indigenous Ahwazis have been reduced to misery, and forced into shanty towns.[30]

Similar treatment has been applied to the Azeris, Baloch, Kurds, and other, smaller groups. Despite Tehran's efforts to convince the world there is a real risk of ethnic separatism, and that without tough action the country might be split apart (a concern often shared by Diaspora Iranians in Europe and the United States), the ethnic groups are overwhelmingly patriotic, and at most ask for moderate rights of the sort that have become common throughout the civilized world: dual language education, some media outlets in their traditional language, and the celebration of traditional holidays.

But the regime, which knows most Iranians despise the mullahs, will not risk even those mild concessions. The regime in Tehran has long since lost any semblance of popular support, and has maintained power only through the systematic use of terror against its people. It cannot claim popularity on the basis of its accomplishments, because twenty-three years of theocracy have produced ruin and misery. Four million people have fled the revolution, most of them well educated and highly skilled. The data on those trapped by the tyrants are startling, but altogether in keeping with the Islamic Revolution's historic indifference to social misery. As Khomeini neatly summarized it, the revolution was about religion, "not about the price of watermelons."[31]

- One-third to one-half of all Iranians are malnourished.
- The average income for more than half the population is $1.40 per day.
- The gross domestic product is less than half of what it was in 1978.
- Per capita income is 7 percent below what it was before the revolution.
- Iranian economists estimate capital flight at up to $3 billion a year, and it may well be significantly greater, as those with money send it to safe havens abroad.
- The country's wealth is firmly in the hands of the regime's elite families. More than 80 percent of the country's gross national product comes from the petroleum industry, which is entirely in government hands. The mullahs have effectively ruined this primary source of national wealth: Oil production is currently around three million barrels per day. It was 6.2 at the end of the shah's rule. According to a study released by the National Academy of Sciences on Christmas Day 2006, oil exports are expected to decline by upwards of 10 percent a year for the foreseeable future.
- According to the International Monetary Fund, Iran requires a crude oil price of at least ninety-five dollars a barrel. The drop in crude prices to below fifty dollars a barrel is very destabilizing, since it seems the Iranian stabilization fund has only enough money to buy imported gasoline for a year, and it may well be even less than that.
- Inflation has run wild. The exchange rate was seventy rials to the dollar in 1978, and it was about 9,300 in the spring of

2007, when a new fifty-thousand rial banknote (graced with an atomic symbol) was introduced.
- Inflation reached nearly 30 percent in October 2008.
- There are said to be more than fifty thousand suicides per year.

With the passage of time, conditions for the Iranian people have steadily worsened, and popular efforts to win even minor concessions—such as the steady tempo of strikes and demonstrations by workers who have not been paid for many months—are crushed with an iron fist. In late November 2008, the leaders of the European Trade Union Confederation and the International Trade Union Confederation wrote to the European Union to ask that the EU intervene on behalf of an Iranian teacher:

> Farzad Kamangar is a thirty-three-year-old teacher and member of the Kurdestan Teachers' Trade Association, and is accused of being a terrorist. According to his lawyer, Khalil Bahramian, there is no evidence to justify the judgement that Mr Kamangar has "endangered national security" or is *moharebe*, "in enmity with God."
>
> Farzad Kamangar's trial was not in accordance with article 168 of the Iranian Constitution: "Political and press offences will be tried openly and in the presence of a jury, in courts of justice." In this case, only one judge reviewed the case within five minutes and the defendant was not allowed to speak. Nevertheless, the death penalty was confirmed by the Supreme Court of Iran on 11 July 2008.

Meanwhile, Kamangar was subjected to ongoing physical and psychological torture, as his cellmates were executed. "[We] have been informed . . . that he has been taken from his cell . . . as a preparation for his execution. . . ." the letter said. "Jail security officers are said to have told him he is about to be executed whilst making fun of him and calling him a martyr."

CORRUPTION

One might expect that Iran would be drowning in wealth, given the enormous increase in oil revenues over the course of the last few years. But that is not the way such societies function. Paul Klebnikov, the intrepid American journalist who specialized in exposing the mafialike activities of post-Soviet Russia—and who was gunned down in Moscow in July 2004—wryly observed,

> The economy bears more than a little resemblance to the crony capitalism that sprouted from the wreck of the Soviet Union. The 1979 revolution expropriated the assets of foreign investors and the nation's wealthiest families; oil had long been nationalized, but the mullahs seized virtually everything else of value—banks, hotels, car and chemical companies, makers of drugs and consumer goods.[32]

Despite Khomeini's celebrated contempt for earthly wealth, the ruling class of the Islamic Republic has demonstrated great avidity for both money and power. The most infamous case is the former president, Ayatollah Ali Akbar Hashemi Rafsanjani, one of the most successful politicians and businessmen, the chairman of the Council of Experts that names the Supreme Leader.

Rafsanjani used the privatization program he launched during his presidency in order to redistribute state-owned enterprises to friends, political allies, and his own family members. The Rafsanjanis were pistachio farmers, and one of Hashemi's brothers now runs a big pistachio export business, estimated at roughly half a billion dollars per year. If you buy pistachios in

Iranian-American shops in Southern California (especially in "Tehrangeles"), the odds are long that you will be enriching the Rafsanjani family fortune.

That is only the beginning. Shortly after the revolution, Rafsanjani family members gobbled up the national television network, created import/export companies, took key positions in the Petroleum Ministry and the organization that builds and manages the Tehran subway system, and even took a thirty-acre horse farm in an upscale neighborhood in the capital (where, according to Klebnikov, land was selling for a cool $4 million per acre).

All that money translates into great political power in a country where most people are struggling to make ends meet. Favors are granted and purchased, networks are established, and the ability to conduct business on an international scale means that money can be salted away in foreign banks as insurance against bad days ahead. Other members of the theocratic ruling class have performed similarly, if less ostentatiously, especially those fortunate enough to have gained control over the national charities or the "bonyads," powerful foundations that in many cases were originally created by the shah's family and were seized after the revolution. All operate under the direct control of the Supreme Leader. The most famous of these is the Mostazafen & Jambazan Foundation, long managed by Mohsen Rafiqdoost, whose main credential was his role as Khomeini's chauffeur on the Imam's triumphal entry into Tehran after the fall of the shah. From there he became minister of the Revolutionary Guards, head of the Mostazafan Foundation, and head of the Noor Foundation, another Islamic "charity" that runs big real estate ventures, imports medicine and other pharmaceutical products, and dabbles in the construction business.

This activity generates enormous sums of money, a large part of which is spent on international terrorism and the country's secret nuclear project. In Klebnikov's words, Iran today is "a dictatorship run by a shadow government that . . . finances terrorist groups abroad through a shadow foreign policy. Its economy is dominated by shadow business empires and its power is protected by a shadow army of enforcers."

Inevitably, the Revolutionary Guards—the main instrument of terror both inside Iran and in the international arena, including Iraq and Afghanistan—realized that it would be more efficient to take direct control over a significant part of the business activities that, after all, provide them with much of their budget. The deputy commander of the IRGC gave a rare public interview in 2006, in which he admitted that nearly one-third of the Guards' operations were not military at all, but commercial, with annual earnings running into the tens of billions of dollars. According to information from well-informed Iranians, as of the start of Operation Iraqi Freedom, the Revolutionary Guards controlled more than thirty companies in Iran and Dubai, through which most of the funding for foreign terrorist operations flowed.

And all of this happened long before oil prices crashed. Whereupon things got considerably worse.

CENSORSHIP

The mullahs have always cracked down on their critics, shutting down any sign of independent political thought, closing newspapers and magazines, and tearing down rooftop satellite dishes that offered Iranians a window into the outside world. These activities have intensified in recent years, prompting one Iranian émigré to remark that "not even the situation in the 1980s and during the Iran-Iraq war rivaled today's."[33]

Whereas in the past, editors and journalists had at least some limited recourse to the court system, by 2007–2008 that had come to an end, and the judiciary joined with the Culture Ministry in suppressing critics of the regime, even when they were associated with legitimate political parties.

By the end of 2008, the regime announced that it had shut down over five million Internet sites, and was requiring all Internet service providers to register with the government so that they could be censored. The Revolutionary Guards' magazine wrote a remarkably candid explanation: The regime feared the free flow of ideas and information to the Iranian people, because if they were well informed, they might rise up against the mullahs.

The Internet, satellite television, and text messages played an important role in the color revolutions in Serbia, Ukraine, and Georgia. Internet search engines Yahoo! and Google, BBC and CNN television, and even international news agencies including Reuters, Associated Press, UPI, AFP, and DPA operated as "tools of diplomacy conducted through the media."[34]

In short, the Iranian regime greatly resembles its totalitarian predecessors of the last century. Patriarchal, xenophobic, relentless in its oppression of those who desire freedom, and brutally destructive of the lives of its own subjects while avid in the pursuit of wealth and power for the tiny ruling elite.

The Ayatollah Khomeini installed a regime in Iran which is best described as Islamic fascism. It is a single-party regime, and a dictator makes all the key decisions. There were endless articles in the press about Mahmoud Ahmadinejad, the current president of Iran, but Iranian presidents come and go. The successor to the Ayatollah Khomeini, Ali Khamenei, has the title of Supreme Leader. He is the only person who really matters in Iran. He makes all the crucial decisions. The Revolutionary Guards Corps reports directly to him.

If you watch Leni Riefenstahl's famous Nazi propaganda film *Triumph of the Will*, about a National Socialist Party day in

Nuremberg, full of *Sieg Heils* and programmed events, you'll see the similarity to those rallies in Tehran where they gather tens of thousands of people to chant "death to America." As with their German and Italian predecessors, the leaders of the Islamic Republic know that mass rallies and collective political rituals do indeed mobilize the masses. As with the Nazis and fascists, the Iranians mean it.

The similarities between the Iranians and the totalitarians of the last century is not at all coincidental, nor is it limited to matters of ritual or the structure of the regimes. Islamic fundamentalism, of which the ideology of the Iranian regime is a textbook case, draws much of its inspiration from Mussolini, Hitler, and Stalin.

There was no European totalitarian movement or regime with which the jihadis were unwilling to collaborate. And although we have heard quite a lot about their collaboration with the Führer (notably in the person of Amin al-Husayni, the wealthy Palestinian landowner who became a violent anti-Semite after reading *The Protocols of the Elders of Zion*, and went on to the office of mufti of Jerusalem), there was a constant, intimate, and extremely important alliance with the Soviet Union that gave some of the key jihadis training in organization (and, undoubtedly, intelligence as well). European Communists were outspoken supporters of the Islamic fanatics, and well before Hitler seized power in Berlin, they excused the Muslims' slaughter of Jews in the Middle East. There were pogroms in Palestine in 1929, and the German Communists supported them, saying "it was a natural development that should not be regretted."[35]

For a while, al-Husayni himself was a Communist of sorts, studying at the feet of the leaders of the Communist Party of Palestine, where he probably picked up such concepts as "imperialism" and "colonialism."

To be sure, the jihadis didn't need Lenin and Stalin to teach them to hate Jews; there was a long history of Islamic anti-Semitism. But they did need Hitler and, more importantly, Himmler, to explain racial doctrine to them and then show them the most modern ways to annihilate the Jews. No surprise that al-Husayni quietly visited Auschwitz with his buddy Adolf Eichmann.

That Islamic fundamentalism was a natural ally of the Third Reich was obvious to some of Hitler's top aides, such as Eichmann and Himmler, but the Führer could never bring himself to endorse Arabs. They were fighting the British, and after all, Hitler believed that the Brits were a "dominant race." The Nazis had an opportunity to embrace the jihadi cause in the summer of 1942, when there were uprisings in India, Iraq, and Iran, but they did not take it, despite the entreaties of al-Husayni and Subhas Chandra Bose. Hitler repeatedly disappointed his Muslim followers, and in his final days he of course blamed it on others, in this case his diplomats, who in reality had been begging him to embrace the jihadis.

> "All Islam vibrated at the news of our victories [in 1940]," he told Bormann in the Berlin bunker. "The Egyptians, the Iraqis and the whole of the Near East were all ready to rise in revolt. Just think what we could have done to help them, even to incite them, as would have been both our duty and our interest."[36]

We should be suitably grateful that Hitler's racism prevented him from vigorously enlisting such potentially valuable allies. Nonetheless, Nazi bureaucrats appreciated the significance of the jihadis, and supported them. Perhaps the most important radical Islamist organization, the violently anti-Semitic Muslim Brotherhood, did receive Nazi assistance, and put it to effective use.

> As the historian Brynjar Lia recounted in his monograph on the Brotherhood, "Documents seized in the flat of Wilhelm Stellbogen, the Director of the German News Agency affiliated to the German Legation in Cairo, show that prior to October 1939 the Muslim Brothers received subsidies from this organization. Stellbogen was instrumental in transferring these funds to the Brothers, which were considerably larger than the subsidies offered to other anti-British activists."[37]

The Nazi true believers recognized kindred spirits when they saw them, just as Mussolini had earlier, when he rhetorically brandished "the sword of Islam" against the British Empire in the Middle East. Among the many things they had in common—Jew-hatred, ideological fanaticism, hatred of the West—one thing in particular should concern anyone committed to the slogan "never again." That is the embrace of death, and the belief that those who love death will inevitably triumph over those who love life more. As a Tunisian intellectual put it on a liberal Middle East Web site, "Why do expressions of tolerance, moderation, rationalism, compromise, and negotiation horrify us [Muslims], but [when we hear] fervent cries for vengeance, we all dance the war dance? . . . Why do other people love life, while we love death and violence, slaughter and suicide, and [even] call it heroism and martyrdom?"[38]

THE CULT OF DEATH

Take Iranian President Mahmoud Ahmadinejad, for example. His adult life has revolved around death. He's from the Revolutionary Guards Corps, the military organization that was created in the Bekáa Valley of Lebanon in the 1970s. The then-incipient Revolutionary Guards were trained there by the expert terrorists of al-Fatah, Yasser Arafat's gang of killers (Sunnis, by the way). One day, the camp was bombed by the Israelis, and a considerable number of his men were killed. Later on, the graduates entered Iran, and killed members of the shah's security forces. Today, Revolutionary Guardsmen crush Iranian dissent at home, and they—the members of the Guards' infamous Quds Force—are on the prowl all over the world, from Iraq and Afghanistan to Buenos Aires, Argentina. So Ahmadinejad has been around death for thirty years or more. Training for it, training others for it, and participating in it.

Ahmadinejad's government spreads death throughout Iranian society, literally carrying the remains of "martyred" fighters onto university campuses and burying them right there. He glorifies death. He thinks it's beautiful. "Art reaches perfection when it portrays the best life and best death," he's said.

> After all, art tells us how to live. That is the essence of art. Is there art that is more beautiful, more divine, and more eternal than the art of martyrdom? A nation with martyrdom knows no captivity. Those who wish to undermine this principle undermine the foundations of our independence and national security. They undermine the foundation of our eternity.

Interestingly, he talks about "independence" and "national security" rather than the interests of Islam, or the Muslim community, or even the Shiites, his sect.

He's a veteran of one of the bloodiest wars of recent times, the Iran-Iraq conflict, which probably cost his country more than a million dead and maimed. He extols that sacrifice, as any patriotic Persian would; Iran was invaded by Saddam Hussein's armies, and the Iranian people defended their country, bravely and desperately.

His praise of Iranian fighters isn't limited to men shot down on the battlefield in that bloody war; he celebrates cases of what he calls—and extols—"martyrdom." It would be more accurate to call it the deliberate, criminal slaughter of many tens of thousands of young children. Some of those kids were twelve years old or younger. They were sent across the battlefields, into Iraqi territory, as human mine detectors. They walked across the minefields and got blown up. The Iraqi soldiers were so horrified that they shouted at the children to stop, to go back. But they didn't; he'd indoctrinated or hypnotized them, and he wanted them to die. Indeed, they were so certain they would be killed that these little children were provided with plastic keys that were said to open the gates to paradise.

In his great work *Crowds and Power,* Elias Canetti explains that those keys had great significance, for they were given to the Shiite martyr Husain.

> . . . the key to Paradise is entrusted him. God himself decrees: "The privilege of intercession is exclusively his. Husain is, by my peculiar grace, the Mediator for all." The prophet Mohammed hands over the key of Paradise to Husain, saying, "Go thou and deliver from the flames everyone who, in his lifetime, has shed by a single tear for thee, everyone who has in any way helped thee, everyone who has performed a pilgrimage to thy shrine, or mourned for thee, everyone who has written tragic verse for thee."[39]

That's not martyrdom; that's mass murder of his own people. Ahmadinejad indoctrinated those kids and sent them to their doom. And it didn't stop with the war. Afterward, the mullahs sent other children to walk across areas they suspected were mined, and many of them were sacrificed in the same way.

This barbarous campaign, of which Ahmadinejad is so proud,

and which he acclaims as a work of art, produced some particularly gruesome technical problems: According to one of Iran's leading newspapers, many of those children were vaporized by the land mines, while others were blown to pieces, their body parts scattered over the earth. The religious leaders insisted that everything be done to keep the bodies intact, and so at a certain point the children were sent to the mine fields wrapped tightly in blankets. Instead of charging bravely to eternity, they rolled across the ground. That way, their cadavers were more likely to hold together, and their families could be given the remains, wrapped in bloody blankets, for burial.

Sending fighters into battles in which their leaders know many, or even most, would die is hardly new. The Russians did it in the First World War, for example, when the second ranks were not armed, but were told that there would be plenty of weapons available; they could just pry them from the hands of their dead comrades. But this massacre of the innocents is something uniquely dreadful.

Ironically, the notion that Muslims love death, thereby gaining an advantage against their life-loving adversaries, was first directed against Ahmadinejad's very own country, Iran itself, during the famous battle at Qadisiyya in 636, between the Muslim armies of Caliph Abu Bakr and the Persians. The Caliph sent a message to the Persians, calling upon them to convert to Islam or pay onerous taxes and accept Muslim rule. Otherwise, he said, "he should know that I have come here with an army of men that love death, as ye love life." (The Muslims won the battle, which marked the end of the Sassanid dynasty in Persia).

Ahmadinejad's praise of the deliberate mass sacrifice of Iran's young, along with his ode to martyrdom, is different from the usual praise of those who make the ultimate sacrifice on behalf of their country or their ideals. It's what the great Spanish philosopher Miguel de Unamuno called "necrophilous" thinking, a pathological love of death. Unamuno used that word in a face-to-face confrontation at the University of Salamanca, where he was the rector, with the famous Spanish general Millán Astray. The Spanish Civil War had just begun, and the general was celebrated in nationalistic circles for his motto *Viva la Muerte*, long live death. The general was an amputee. Unamuno noted that the great Spanish writer Cervantes was also handicapped, and continued, "It pains me to think that General Millán Astray should dictate the pattern of mass psychology. A cripple who lacks the spiritual greatness of a Cervantes is wont to seek ominous relief in causing mutilation around him." Unamuno denounced "long live death" as a "necrophilous and senseless cry."

Today, the mullahs and the other jihadis are in the same position as General Millán Astray. Their celebration of death is as necrophilous as the general's. This is not a philosophical matter, despite Ahmadinejad's efforts to elevate it to the stature of aesthetics. It's a disease, with well-known symptoms and consequences. People like he, who are fascinated by death, are terribly destructive of others and themselves.

Necrophilia is defined as "the passionate attraction to all that is dead, decayed, putrid, sickly; it is the passion to transform that which is alive into something unalive; to destroy for the sake of destruction. . . . It is the passion to tear apart living structures." That is the language Ahmadinejad uses, especially about the Jews, the Israelis, and the Americans. It's all about the rot of death, and the stink of death, as when he said that Israel is a "rotten and stinking corpse" that is destined to disappear, and went on to proclaim that Israel "has reached the end like a dead rat."

It's a textbook case of mental illness. And we're very well acquainted with the political consequences of the diseased mind. It's all about fascism.

Fascists like Ahmadinejad always love death. Hitler's SS had a death skull on their insignia, and celebrated a brave death.

Like Hitler, the Iranians don't just love death because of its aesthetics. They think that martyrs—suicide bombers, of whom he claims to have recruited some forty thousand, for example—have geopolitical significance. He says that "all independent nations are indebted to martyrs," and his Web site modestly claims that the oppressed peoples of the world all love Iran's leaders, particularly himself and Supreme Leader Ali Khamenei.

The jihadis' necrophilia is not merely a matter of ideology or personal perversity; it is very much present in their actions, in the evils they perform whenever they can.

It is also a method of indoctrinating and repressing would-be dissidents. As Amil Imani notes, when the regime brings the bodies of the martyrs onto university campuses, they probably have two distinct, but closely related, purposes in mind:

> . . . one way to interpret this situation is the regime's way to impose on the university milieu and student life a militant ideology that praises *shahâdat* (the martyr death), endless war and military values accompanied by the Islamic Revolutionary Guards and the eulogizing of the eight-year war with Iraq.
>
> It is also an Orwellian tactic for the militia groups (Basijis) to clamp down on student gatherings and demonstrations. It is an invasion of personal privacy, either directly physically or indirectly by surveillance. It is an Islamic way of controlling its citizens' daily life, as in "Big Brother" is watching you. It is the Islamic republic's strategy to suppress dissident voices within Iran's lively university environment.[40]

In both cases, the cult of death is central to the mission of the regime, as it is to radical Islamic terrorists all over the world. The jihadis—not just the suicide terrorists, but also those who kill and then live to kill another day—share in the passion to transform living men into corpses. Take, for example, the assassination of Jordanian Prime Minister Wasfi al-Tal at the Sheraton hotel in Cairo in November 1971:

> "Five . . . shots, fired at point-blank range. . . . He staggered back against the shattered swing doors . . . and he fell dying among the shards of glass on the marble floor. As he lay there, one of his killers bent over and lapped the blood that poured from his wounds."[41]

When the Iraqi monarchy was overthrown in 1958, the cadaver of the deposed king's uncle was turned over to the bloodlust of the people: "His body was dismembered with axes and his limbs and head tossed about by the hysterical mob. The trunk was hung from a balcony and chunks of his flesh were sliced off and thrown to the crowd below."[42] This sort of horror is neither rare nor a source of embarrassment to men like Ahmadinejad, Khamenei, and their comrades. Gruesome torture and murder (such as beheadings) are celebrated, not hidden. The beheading of Daniel Pearl was proudly circulated to the world—especially to other jihadi terrorists and potential recruits—and the Jewish victims of the November 2008 terror assault in Mumbai, India, were tortured before being executed. Beheadings are particularly useful for recruiting new terrorists, who love the bloody spectacle and wish to participate in it.

Nor is such savagery limited to the "holy war" on infidels. If anything, it is visited more often on fellow Muslims. The Saudis, for example, routinely behead those convicted of capital offenses—more than a thousand have been decapitated in the past two decades. Sometimes the intent is clearly the same as the terrorists': to frighten their enemies. In 1979, for example, one Juhayman al-Otaibi led a revolt against the royal family, declaring his brother-in-law to be the rightful leader of the Muslim people. He and his followers occupied the mosque in

Mecca and called for the overthrow of the Saudis. The uprising was quashed, and all rebel survivors were publicly beheaded.

Blood rituals are especially popular in Iran. There is a martyrs' fountain in Tehran, where the liquid is tinted the color of blood, and the most intense religious celebration in Iranian Shiism, the *Ashura,* commemorates the murder of Husayn. On that day, religious men parade through the streets, lashing themselves with metal-tipped whips that draw blood, which then flows over their bodies. Gobineau witnessed the spectacle, and wrote about it in shocked detail:

> 500,000 people, seized with madness, cover their heads with ashes and beat their foreheads on the ground. They want to give themselves up to torture, to commit suicide in groups, or to mutilate themselves . . . several will be dead by evening, and many more mutilated and disfigured; their shirts, red with blood, will be their shrouds. They are beings who have already ceased to belong to this world.[43]

Shiite Islam is a religion of lament and mourning, but it is also very much a religion of war. A few days before Yitzhak Rabin and Yasser Arafat shook hands on the White House lawn, aides to President Clinton called the great scholar Bernard Lewis for help with Clinton's speech. Could Lewis provide them with a good quotation praising peace from the Koran? Lewis quoted them one from memory. "No, we've already used that one," he was told. "We need a different one." But Lewis had to tell them that, so far as he knew, that was the only one. So, while martyrdom and self-flagellation are admirable as acts of faith, death in battle—death while waging jihad—is much better.

Thus violence against men, women, and children is routinely approved by high religious and secular leaders, and the killers are hailed as heroes. We should not be misled by all the talk about "martyrdom." The point is killing the enemy.

We should not be misled about the cunning of the mullahs. Despite Ahmadinejad's hymn to death, he and his fellow Iranian leaders don't actually fight. They inspire jihad, but they do not wage it themselves. With the exception of the Revolutionary Guards Corps in Iraq and Afghanistan, very few Iranians put themselves on the line (and even the foreign legions rarely fight; when they are captured, they often give us the information we need to defeat them, as we have in Iraq). They lure others to die, but they're not willing to put their own lives on the line. Ahmadinejad talks a lot about the "culture of martyrdom," but in practice it's not Iranians who blow themselves up. I don't know of a single case of an Iranian suicide bomber in Iraq or Afghanistan. They're all Arabs: Saudis, North Africans, and the odd Syrian fanatic. But not Iranians. All of which suggests that the big talk about martyrdom is for others—in the current campaign, others Ahmadinejad and most other Iranians despise, like the Arabs. They're not about to blow themselves up, or send their comrades to blow themselves up.

Ahmadinejad has won the status of the world's leading anti-Semite, which is not easy, and he's lied about it a lot. Indeed, he has denied—on CBS television—hating any religion, which is manifestly false; he's been seen on Iranian TV spouting venom against all non-Muslims, with special contempt for Christians and Jews. But when he talks to the infidels, he pretends to be tolerant. For a guy who has distinctly medieval convictions—his very literal belief in the imminent return of the Shiite messiah, the Twelfth Imam, and the onset of the End of Days, for example—he's certainly mastered some of the nuances of contemporary Western politics. He never chants, "Death to the Jews!" It's always "Death to Israel!" Or "Death to the Zionists!" Or "Death to America!"

That's entirely in keeping with the "new" anti-Semitism. It's always about Zionists, or the Israel lobby, or the lackeys of Sharon. But every now and then he just can't resist, and out it comes. Instead of remembering to say that he respects all monotheistic religions, he tells his followers, "We are in the process of a historical war between the World of Arrogance and the Islamic world, and this war has been going on for hundreds of years." Zionists haven't been around that long. His comrades aren't nearly as careful with their language as he usually is. The Iranian creation Hezbollah told us in 1992 that they were engaged in "an open war until the elimination of Israel and until the death of the last Jew on earth." Ten years later, the leader of the "Party of God," Lebanese Sheikh Nasrallah, was quoted by the Lebanese *Daily Star,* encouraging all the Jews to move to Israel, the better to annihilate them in one blow. "If they all gather in Israel, it will save us the trouble of going after them worldwide." And of course, Osama bin Laden himself declared in 1998, "The enmity between us and the Jews goes back far in time and is deep-rooted. There is no question that war between us is inevitable. . . . The Hour of Resurrection shall not come before Muslims fight Jews."[44]

Ahmadinejad's senior adviser Mohammad Ali Ramin (said to be the man behind the infamous Holocaust Denial Conference), says the Jews have been accused of spreading deadly plagues throughout history because "they are very filthy people." And, almost in the same breath, he added, "So long as Israel exists in the region there will never be peace and security in the Middle East . . . so the resolution of the Holocaust issue will end in the destruction of Israel."

In its report on global anti-Semitism for 2003–2004, the Department of State noted that "many newspapers celebrated the 100th anniversary of the publication of the anti Semitic 'The Protocols of the Elders of Zion.' Recent demonstrations have included the denunciations of 'Jews,' as opposed to the past practice of denouncing only 'Israel' and 'Zionism' . . ."[45]

That Iranians are engaged in a global campaign to destroy the Jews is evident from their actions as well as their words; Hezbollah and the Iranian regime were joint partners in the bombing of the Jewish Social Center in Buenos Aires in 1994.

There's obviously a big difference for Ahmadinejad between dead Muslims and dead Jews. Only his dead count; the victims don't qualify as martyrs. This is the point of his infamous diatribes against the very idea of the Holocaust. "[The Zionists and their agents] have concocted a myth of deprivation and innocence for the Jews of Europe," he's said. "They use this pretext of the innocence of Jews and the suffering of some Jews during the Second World War . . ."

Despite his claim to devote his life to the triumph of the Shiite vision, Ahmadinejad's description of his mission is often at odds with the core of Khomeinist doctrine. He's proclaimed Iran "the most powerful and independent country in the world." The implication of that grandiose claim is that the weaker and dependent nations—that is, everyone else in the world—must bend to Iran's will. He's said this more than once, and in somewhat different ways, as when he said that the Iranian people must prepare themselves to rule the world.

Those statements are very surprising, coming from one of the leaders of the Islamic Republic of Iran. Those words put him in direct conflict with the founder of the Islamic Republic, Ayatollah Ruhallah Khomeini. On the Air France plane carrying him from Paris to Tehran, Khomeini famously proclaimed that nationalism was paganism, that he didn't give a hoot about Iran, and that his revolution was for all of Islam, not for one country. Indeed, if Iran perished in order to advance the global triumph of Islam, it would be fine with him.

So Ahmadinejad's claim of Iranian supremacy would seem to

be heretical. He constantly claims to be the heir to Khomeini, a true believer in the imminent return of the Twelfth Imam, but as a matter of fact he embraces a heretical doctrine. The Twelfth Imam is supposed to bring about the global triumph of the Muslim people, not a hegemonic Iran. And another thing: He often talks as if global chaos and conflagration were welcome, because it would hasten the *Mahdi*'s arrival. But Khomeini did not say that, nor did he act as if he believed it. Quite the contrary, in fact: When an Iranian passenger plane was accidentally shot down by an American missile, he didn't welcome it at all; he surrendered. One American missile ended the Iran-Iraq War.

It's worth keeping that in mind as we ponder our response to the Iranian evil. But first we have to understand it. The first step is to acknowledge that the evil lies within all of us, that we are capable of such beliefs, such passions—including the seemingly alien bloodlust—and such actions. The true horror of fascism—which in many ways is the real model for today's terror masters—is precisely its popular success. It's not just that people accept it or endure it; they often embrace it and celebrate it. The terrorists who attacked us on September 11, 2001, did not come out of religious schools, did not grow up in a religious atmosphere, and did not emerge from social or economic misery. They embraced jihadism freely; it was a free choice that gave meaning to their lives.

The first great scholar of totalitarianism, Hannah Arendt, groped toward understanding, and she can help us do the same today:

> That man may lose his identity without knowing it, that Fascism may be the loss of one's sense of self and hence the loss of all sense of limitations, is for Arendt the psychological terror of Fascism. And conversely, to refuse to accept man's finite condition, to succumb to the seductive totality

> of ideology in the face of the dizzy chaos of history, to strive for essence in defiance of the enigma of existence, is the metaphysical dread of Fascism.[46]

Today's Islamofascism is very much in that tradition. It has a lot of popular support, as we saw both in elections in Egypt and Gaza and in the jihadi terror organizations, as we saw in the past in Algeria and in the Iranian Revolution of 1979. We are now threatened by an Islamic version of totalitarianism that we prefer not see, just as in the fascist era and again with regard to Soviet Communism. We're going to have to see it, understand it, and then vanquish it.

3

TO SEE EVIL

The problem is not that the Islamists hide their goals. The problem is that the West does not listen. Osama bin Laden's chief reproach of the Americans in his "Letter to the American People" is that they act as free citizens who make their own laws instead of accepting sharia. The same hatred of freedom can be found in Mahmoud Ahmadinejad's letter to the American president: "Those with insight can already hear the sounds of the shattering and fall of the ideology and thoughts of the liberal democratic systems."

—Matthias Küntzel

Our present enemies express themselves in the language of Islam, and there is a considerable literature that traces the jihadis' hatred of the West, of Christianity, and of the Jews back to the Koran. The authors of these books and articles are no doubt correct when they say—as students of Islam have said for many centuries—that the Prophet Mohammed was a warrior, and that one of the principal goals of the religion he passed on to the faithful was the destruction and subjection of the infidels. It is hard to read the Koran otherwise, when it explicitly says,

"When the sacred months are over, slay the idolaters wherever you find them. Arrest them, besiege them and lie in ambush for them."[1] There are many other passages exhorting the faithful to kill their enemies, and precious little about the virtues of the peacemakers.

Moreover, Islam has not had the sort of authoritative, ongoing interpretation that has played such an important role in the two other major monotheistic religions, Judaism and Christianity. There is no Muslim equivalent of the Jewish Mishnah or Talmud, no Muslim equivalent of the doctrinal battles in Christian Europe during the Middle Ages, nothing like the Council of Trent or the more recent Vatican Councils, and certainly nothing remotely approaching the Protestant Reformation. Islamic fundamentalists will tell you that the Koran is the final and complete revelation of God's message to man. When asked about the laws of the new Islamic Republic of Iran, the Ayatollah Khomeini responded contemptuously, "You have no need for new legislation; simply put into effect that which has already been legislated for you"—the holy law, the sharia.

Islam has traditionally been so rigid that one scholar, very favorably inclined toward the religion and toward Muslim causes, called it "totalitarian" in its very essence.

> Islam has been totalitarian to an extreme. Indeed, in principle, it dominated every act and every thought of the faithful. . . . All actions, even those arising out of the most elementary biological needs, such as excretion and coition, were regulated by the ideological system.[2]

Nonetheless, all ideas change over time, even those (like those contained in the Koran) that are believed to have been dictated by God's angel. The current Islamist doctrine—the views famously expressed by Osama bin Laden or Ali Khamenei—is far more than the repetition of medieval commandments, and the lack of a single authoritative voice (such as the Pope) means that local religious leaders issue opinions or rulings whose legitimacy can be challenged by other imams or mullahs.

So on the one hand, there can be no reinterpretation of the Koran, but on the other hand, specific guidance based upon it is wildly decentralized, and subject to individual eccentricities. And there is a certain amount of room for at least some change, some "renovation." There is a collection of Mohammad's wise sayings, known as hadith, and two of them point to the possibility of new Muslim insights. The first says, "Allah will send [to the Muslims] at the advent of every hundred years a person [or persons] who will renovate its religion." The second promises that "at the end of every century, Almighty Allah will send such a person . . . who will revive the religion."[3]

The theoretical limits of interpreting the Koran were quite strict, and for a long time the very idea of an Islamic "revolution" seemed oxymoronic. As Bernard Lewis wrote in the early 1970s, Muslims could rebel, they could even participate in insurrections, but could not participate in a revolution.[4]

Nonetheless, rather like the dear bumblebee—which generations of mechanical engineers said could not fly because of the relationship between wing span and body mass, but which, unaware of the science, flew anyway—twentieth-century Muslims studied the question of revolution, and some of them found ways to graft radical Western doctrines onto the Koran.

One example is particularly important: the case of the Pakistani Sayyid Abul Ala Maududi, a friend of Khomeini and of Sayyid Qutb (the spiritual guru of Osama bin Laden). Maududi's worldview was a mishmash of millenarian visions accompanied by cries for social justice, combining Islamic and Marxist language. Like Khomeini's vision, Maududi's claims were universal: "Islam addresses its call for effecting [its] program of destruction and reconstruction, revolution and reform not to just one nation, but to all humanity," and he went so far as to assert that "the acid test of the true devotion" of the believer is that he commits himself to world revolution. "Islam wishes to destroy all states and governments on the face of the earth which are opposed to the ideology and program of Islam regardless of the country."[5]

Maududi had an enormous appreciation of his own talents, believing that he could sense the thinking of Mohammed far beyond the words of the hadith. "Upon seeing a *hadith*, I can tell whether the Holy Prophet could or could not have said it," and he believed he was one of those rare people sent by Allah once a century to guide the faithful. He did not consider himself a prophet, but did think he came "very close to prophethood . . . [with] power to think independently of the contemporary and centuries-old social and other prejudices, courage to fight against the evils of the time, inherent ability to lead and guide."[6]

Maududi remains enormously important in the Islamist movement. His ideas are canonical for the Jamaat al-Islami, which is very active in Britain, especially in the Islamic Foundation in Leicester.[7]

In this manner, various Islamic leaders—of whom Khomeini has been the most important—folded some very Western ideas about revolution into their religious worldview. And why not? One of the keys to the success of modern mass movements was the creation of a "secular religion," and leaders of the totalitarian states of the twentieth century often developed political rituals that captured the sort of enthusiasm traditionally generated in religious observance. The Muslim revolutionaries already had the religious component, the rituals, and the enthusiasm, which they put to work in support of the revolution, fascist- or communist-inspired as the case may have been.

This was particularly true in the Iranian Revolution, for the

Shiite belief that the Twelfth Imam (aka the *Mahdi*, or "Imam of the Age") would emerge from "occultation" in a Persian well, and lead the Shiites to global triumph, was a perfect fit with calls for revolution and the creation of an Islamic Republic that would eventually dominate the world.

No wonder, then, that 5 percent of the Iranian electorate—four hundred thousand voters—voted for the Twelfth Imam in the presidential elections of 1981. The messianic figure has remained hyperactive in Iranian politics, especially during the presidency of Mahmoud Ahmadinejad. When his government first met, Ahmadinejad required them all to sign a contract with the "Imam of the Age," and the official document was then carried to the well so the Shiite Messiah could read it.

Many Iranian leaders are quite explicit in their belief that the Twelfth Imam is getting restless in his well, and will soon climb out into the sunlight of the apocalypse. Ahmadinejad is forever calling attention to signs and portents of the *Mahdi*'s emergence. Speaking in the holy city of Mashhad in November 2008, he put it this way: "Grandees [of the faith] have told us that one of the signs of realization of that important and great promise which is emergence of His Holiness the Mahdi—May God hasten his emergence—is whispering of his name globally. Let me tell you this, thanks to your tears and prayers . . . hearts of humanity are turning towards the Imam [of the Era] fast."

As you might expect, this sort of fever spreads wide and fast, sometimes in ways the regime does not much like.[8] A couple of news flashes from mid-November 2008 indicate the sort of thing that erupts among the faithful:

- Mostafa Barzegar Ganji, public prosecutor of Qom, reports the arrest and imprisonment of five men who claim to be Imam of the Era. Barzegar also reports a man claiming to be the "fourteenth Imam of the Shi'as" has been imprisoned.

- Ali-Reza Peyghan, who says he is Imam of the Era and author to the 673-page Al-Qa'em, and who gained fame by praying with his face turned towards the mosque of Jamkaran, is to be hanged.[9]

In keeping with their embrace of some of the main themes of European and Russian totalitarianism, blended with the revealed truths of the Koran and the hadith, the leaders of the Islamic Republic are quite outspoken about the nature of the apocalyptic struggle in which they are engaged. They believe that the final battle will be fought between the followers of the Twelfth Imam and the Jews and their followers, in Israel, America, and the West.

On November 16, 2006, Mohammed Hassan Rahimian, a close associate of Supreme Leader Khamenei, said, "The Jew is the most stubborn enemy of the believer. And the decisive war will decide the fate of humanity. . . . The reappearance of the Twelfth Imam will usher in a war between Israel and the Shia."[10]

Mehdi Khalaji, who studied for fourteen years in theological seminaries in the holy city of Qom, Iran, notes a June 26, 2007, speech by Ahmadinejad in which he publicly warned Israel that the millenium was coming, and his arrival would signify the end of Israel: "All the world sees that you are going to be marked, because justice and the pioneer of justice is on his way." Khalaji goes on, "Ahmadinejad appears to be influenced by a trend in contemporary apocalyptic thought in which the killing of Jews will be one of the most significant accomplishments of the Mahdi's government."[11] Just a couple of months later, Ahmadinejad told the United Nations General Assembly, "The age of darkness will end . . . the peoples in Europe and America will be liberated from the burdens the Zionists have inflicted on them."

The Twelfth Imam will not only lead the destruction of the infidels, but he will also open the gates of Paradise to the believers. There, the faithful—and above all, the martyrs—will truly be rewarded, with sexual ecstasy that has been denied them on this earth:[12]

When We Meet the Black-Eyed Virgin

Omar Al-Sweilem: "Harith Ibn Al-Muhasibi told us what would happen when we meet the black-eyed virgin with her black hair and white face—praised be He who created night and day.

"What hair! What a chest! What a mouth! What cheeks! What a figure! What breasts! What thighs! What legs! What whiteness! What softness! Without any creams—no Nivea, no Vaseline. No nothing!"

"You Would Find 10 Black-Eyed Virgins Sprawled on Musk Cushions"

"He said that faces would be soft that day. Even your own face will be soft without any powder or makeup. You yourself will be soft, so how soft will a black-eyed virgin be, when she comes to you so tall and with her beautiful face, her black hair and white face—praised be He who created night and day. Just feel her palm, Sheikh!

"He said: How soft will a fingertip be, after being softened in paradise for thousands of years! There is no god but Allah. He told us that if you entered one of the palaces, you would find 10 black-eyed virgins sprawled on musk cushions. Where is Abu Khaled? Here, he has arrived!

"When they see you, they will get up and run to you. Lucky is the one who gets to put her thumb in your hand. When they get hold of you, they will push you onto your

> back, on the musk cushions. They will push you onto your back, Jamal! Allah Akbar! I wish this on all people present here.
>
> "He said that one of them would place her mouth on yours. Do whatever you want.
>
> "Another one would press her cheek against yours, yet another would press her chest against yours, and the others would await their turn. There is no god but Allah."
>
> **Wine in Paradise Is a Reward for Your Good Deeds**
>
> "He told us that one black-eyed virgin would give you a glass of wine. Wine in Paradise is a reward for your good deeds. The wine of this world is destructive, but not the wine of the world to come."

Meanwhile, in the earthly Islamic Republic, the mullahs continue to crack down on "satanic clothing,"[13] arresting women who permit others to see at least the outlines of their bodies, men who wear fashionable spiked hairdos, and barbers who do their satanic work. Among its many other dreadful attributes, the Iranian regime has long declared war against fun inside its borders. Supreme Leader Khamenei made a name for himself a couple of decades ago by delivering a resounding denunciation of music, after all.

Iran is waging war against the West both for old, fundamental Islamic motives and also for many of the same reasons the Nazis, fascists, and Communists attacked us. The combination of religious fanaticism, with its explicitly apocalyptic promise of Paradise for the true believers and death and damnation for their enemies, and revolutionary political ideology inspires terrorist organizations like Hamas, Hezbollah, and al Qaeda to target both infidels and insufficiently observant Muslims.

When Bernard-Henri Lévy wrote his important book[14] about

Omar Sheikh, the British man who slaughtered *Wall Street Journal* journalist Daniel Pearl in Sheikh's native Pakistan, he saw firsthand the nature of the evil that confronts us. "There is floating around, in these cities, the odor of apocalypse," he writes. And as he traces Omar Sheikh's steps from the best British schools and universities to the killing fields of the Middle East, Lévy finds that Sheikh simply passed from being a good bourgeois gentleman to a bloodthirsty killer, driven by hate for America, hate for the West, perhaps anger over the fate of Kashmir, and at bottom, hate for the Jews. Lévy was shocked to discover such intense anti-Semitism, not only in Sheikh but among a big swath of the Pakistani people, even though very few of them had ever had contact with Jews, or for that matter knew anything much about them (no one seems to have recognized that Lévy's surname was a dead giveaway to his ethnicity). Lévy confessed to real fear that he'd be killed if the wrong person discovered he was Jewish; he'd realized that the hatred of Daniel Pearl could just as easily be directed against a French Jew.

> Pearl died for being an American in a country where to be an American is a sin that is not unlike, in the rhetoric that stigmatizes him, the sin of being Jewish. Pearl was the victim of that other vile stupidity called anti-Americanism that makes one, in the eyes of these neo-fascists that are the Islamicists, a reject, a sub-human to eliminate. American, thus bad. America, or Evil. The old Western anti-Americanism crossed with that of these fanatics of God. The rancid hatred of our Pétainists, restyled for the Third World and the wretched of the Earth.

Lévy goes on to describe what he calls "new anti-Semitism," or, more grandiosely, "a neo-anti-Judaism that is emerging before our eyes. . . . We are in the process of seeing a new purity of blood . . . a new formulation, a new way of justifying the worst that . . . at a global scale, associates the hatred of Jews with the defense of the oppressed."

Actually, there is precious little "new" or "neo" in the Jew-hatred that inspires men like Omar Sheikh, or with the theory that the Jews are responsible for the misery of the world's poor. This has been a central theme of Western anti-Semitism for centuries. The only "new" element is the obsession with Israel, the Jewish state. But the Iranians make it quite clear that Israel is the least of their hatreds; Israel is only the "little Satan." The "great Satan" is America. We, and our Western allies, are their ultimate enemies, and their preferred targets. Just ask the people of Mumbai, India. Or ask Ed Husain, the repentant British Islamist who ran away from a radical Islamist movement in which he had worked for years. "We were talking of crusades long before George W. Bush," he laconically notes in his autobiography. "Muslims in [the crusader countries] had an ideological duty to unite behind the Islamic state and be prepared to launch attacks on Britain from within."[15]

Like the other totalitarian movements, radical Islam wants to create a new order (or, if you prefer, restore an old order) in which all mankind will be governed by those most suitable for leadership. All contemporary issues, even the ones that most agitate us, from social justice at home to a fair international order, are utterly secondary to them. Everything they do must support the mission, which is the same as it has been all along: dominate or destroy their enemies.

Lévy well understands the totalitarian impulse within the dark hearts of the jihadis, but even he does not recognize the flimsiness of the lines that divide fascists, Nazis, Communists, and Islamists. The labels suggest an impermeability that does not exist in practice. Robert Conquest mused on the frequency with which loyal Communists came to support Hitler, a phenomenon the Führer understood quite well.

> Everywhere we come across the ease with which people passed from Communism to what were in theory its most virulent enemies—Fascism and National Socialism. Several Italian Fascist leaders, like Bombacci, had held positions in the Comintern—as had Jacques Doriot in France, who even led a French pro-Nazi military formation on the Eastern Front in World War II.
>
> Hitler himself said that Communists far more easily became Nazis than Social Democrats.[16]

The same was true in Italy. Mussolini himself and many of his comrades were former Socialists, after all, and, especially in the early years of his rule, he attracted many radicals, including anarcho-syndicalists, to the ranks of the Fascist Party. If you look at the propaganda of the so-called Republic of Salò, the statelet in Northern Italy created for him by the Nazis after the fall of fascism, you will find all manner of left-wing language, and some of the intellectuals who rallied round *Il Duce* did so in the belief that he was finally going to carry out a real social revolution.

Many of those fascists, including some of the worst anti-Semites, proclaimed themselves "people of the left" after the war, and most of them joined the Communist Party, which provided them intellectual protection in return for their loyalty. In recent years, Italians have started to look much more objectively at their fascist past[17] and the immediate postwar period, and have called attention to two ugly facts: First, Italian fascist anti-Semitism was much nastier and much more widespread than had previously been acknowledged; and second, after the Second World War, the

Communist Party covered up the anti-Semitic activities of those intellectuals and young politicians who cooperated with the Communists.

> . . . the famous Marxist philosopher Galvano Della Volpe in 1940 . . . praised the "glorious humanism" of Goethe, Nietzsche, and Mussolini, while lamenting the degree to which Jews had corrupted modern thought. The noted archeologist Ranuccio Bianchi Bandinelli, who later became a communist and director of the Gramsci Institute, was photographed in full fascist regalia, guiding Mussolini and Hitler through the latter's visit in 1938. There were also viciously antisemitic articles written by the noted journalist Giorgio Bocca and the future prime minister Giovanni Spadolini.[18]

The list of Italian fascists, including some of the most outspoken anti-Semites, comes close to constituting a postwar Who's Who of the journalistic and university intellectual elite. To be sure, a certain number of these people moved from right to left for purely opportunistic or pragmatic motives. But the leaders of the Communist Party believed that a significant number of "fascists in good faith" were motivated by many of the same ideals as the Communists, and gave instructions to the Underground to try to recruit such people. Testimony to this effect comes from Giorgio Amendola, a longtime member of the Italian Communist Politburo.[19]

Radical extremists of whatever color have more in common than is generally acknowledged, and, especially in the past hundred or more years, anti-Semitism has proven attractive to almost all of them. At her trial, the left-wing "revolutionary" terrorist Ulrike Meinhof openly stated that "Auschwitz meant that six million Jews were killed, and thrown onto the wasteheap of Europe for what they were: money-Jews [*Geldjuden*]."[20]

And when a British observer wondered how it could be that the famous French lawyer Jacques Vergès could defend killers ranging from Klaus Barbie (the "butcher of Lyons" during the Vichy period) and the celebrity terrorist "Carlos the Jackal" to members of the Baader-Meinhof group, Tariq Aziz from Saddam's regime, and numerous Palestinian terrorists, a Conservative member of Parliament thought he saw a connection.

> What is it that has marked the most sustained terror campaign in the Middle East? What was it that characterised Barbie's period in charge of security in wartime Lyons? What drove the arguments made by those survivors of the Baader-Meinhof gang who are still politically active today, such as Horst Mahler? And what tie binds Carlos the Jackal, the renegade terrorist of the 1970s, to Tariq Aziz, the Establishment face of prewar Iraq?
>
> One thing unites them all: anti-Semitism. While Stourton might have found it hard to see what united Palestinian terrorists and Klaus Barbie, it was instantly apparent to me—both made the elimination of Jewish lives a central ideological mission. Just as Carlos the Jackal did in the 1970s, when he launched rocket attacks on El Al airlines and targeted Jewish businessmen. And just as Tariq Aziz did in the 1990s, when Iraqi Scud missiles were directed against Israel, and Iraqi money subsidised suicide bombing.[21]

It's quite an old story, and it helps us understand the ability of the Iranian regime to gain support (or, at a minimum, induce benign neglect) from political and intellectual groups in the West at both ends of the political spectrum, as well as from the Islamists. From Khomeini on, Iranians have been quite willing to form alliances with countries, groups, and movements that would seem to be totally unacceptable to a regime motivated solely by Koranic texts and wise sayings from the Prophet Mohammed. The Iranians have created a network of strategic alliances that stretches from the Middle East to Latin America, best symbolized by the frequent flights of Iran Air planes between Iran, Syria, and Venezuela. As usual, the prime instrument of Iranian power is Hezbollah, and as always, Hezbollah spreads terror instruments and the Shiite faith. Thousands of Latin Americans are now converting to Shiite Islam, and in Venezuela one such convert, a man who calls himself "Commander Teodoro," publicly warned that in the event of an American attack against Iran, "the only country ruled by God, we would counterattack in Latin America and even inside the United States itself. We have the means and we know how to go about it. We will sabotage the transportation of oil from Latin America to the U.S. You have been warned."[22]

Hezbollah's activities attracted the attention of the United States Treasury Department, which seized the assets of two Hezbollah "facilitators," believed to be laundering money for terrorists. Treasury's Adam Szubin made it clear that the department's Office of Foreign Assets Control did not think this was a rogue operation; he spoke of "the government of Venezuela employing and providing safe harbor to Hezbollah facilitators and fundraisers." The deputy director of national intelligence, Don Kerr, pointed to cooperation between Hezbollah and narcoterrorists. "In Latin America you see the conjunction of narcotics trafficking and terrorism, and there may be a nexus forming between them," said Kerr. "They share the need for money laundering. In fact in Latin America you have a real presence of Hezbollah."[23]

The two Hezbollah activists designated as terror elements by the U.S. Treasury are alleged to have "facilitated the travel" of Hezbollah members to and from Venezuela and to a "training course in Iran." Treasury officials also formally accused Ghazi Nasr al Din of exploiting his positions at Venezuelan embassies in the Middle East (in Syria and Lebanon) and his status as president of a Shia Muslim center in Caracas to support financing for Hezbollah. According to the U.S. Treasury, Nasr al Din advised donors on financial contributions to Hezbollah, and provided them with the numbers of specific bank accounts into which to deposit the funds.

Nasr al Din is also alleged to have met with senior Hezbollah officials to "discuss operational issues." He is believed to have helped Hezbollah activists to travel to and from Venezuela; and in January 2006, he arranged for two Hezbollah members of the Lebanese parliament to travel to Venezuela for a fund-raising drive and to dedicate a Hezbollah-supported community center.

In mid-July 2006, *El Universal* newspaper's Web site exposed intelligence information from the U.S. Drug Enforcement Administration that claimed that members of the Gulf and Sinaloa Mexican drug cartels were being sent to Iran to be trained in the use of explosives and as snipers by the ubiquitous Revolutionary Guards. According to the sources, the drug cartel members were traveling from Mexico to Venezuela and then on to Iran in weekly flights to Tehran. In some cases, the sources said, the drug cartel members were traveling on Venezuelan passports. According to the newspaper, a number of "Lebanese terrorists who belong to Iran [Hezbollah]" have managed to secure Mexican citizenship by way of marriages arranged by drug cartels in the country.

Police in Ecuador reported in the fall of 2008 that they had apprehended members of an international drug-smuggling network that was "funding" Hezbollah. Authorities in Ecuador refused to provide details on the alleged ties between the drug network and Hezbollah, but noted that the drug network had transferred 70 percent of its profits to the Lebanon-based group. Senior Ecuadorian officials identified the leader of the drug network as the owner of a Lebanese restaurant in the capital, Quito.

Venezuelan dictator Hugo Chávez has become an enthusiastic friend of Ahmadinejad, and the two countries have joint projects too numerous to list, from oil development and nuclear energy to public works and greatly expanded military spending. And not surprisingly, in addition to their mutual hatred of America, they are at one in hatred of the Jews. Chávez's Jew-hatred is a mixture of traditional Catholic anti-Semitism, resting on the accusation that the Jews killed Christ, and populist left-wing anti-Jewish rhetoric, accusing them of causing impoverishment and seizing control of the world's wealth.[24] And along with Chávez, we can now add Evo Morales in Bolivia (a frequent traveler to Libya, Syria, and Iran), and, of course, the Castro brothers in Havana.

So Iran is a major threat to the West, even aside from its race to develop nuclear weapons, and the mullahs make little effort to conceal their intentions from us. Anyone who spends a few hours reading the statements of Iranian leaders will find much of it, and the rest is readily available in scholarly texts. Iran's regime is every bit as monstrous and every bit as dangerous as the totalitarian regimes of the past century, and it is no accident that it has placed Jew-hatred at the center of its creed.

IRAN AND THE AMERICAN MEDIA

You might think that Iran would be a major subject of investigative journalism, but like the totalitarian regimes of the last century, it has been surprisingly free of major exposés in the mainstream press, at least in the United States (the German press, especially *Der Spiegel*, has been better). Indeed, in some cases, the press coverage of Iran is uncomfortably reminiscent of *The New York Times*'s failure to present an accurate picture of events in communist and fascist countries. From surprisingly positive coverage of Iran's tyrannical leaders, to "reporting" designed to thwart any American inclination to support Iranian dissidents, American readers—unless they are very skilled and careful readers—are unlikely to realize that Iran's leaders are committed to the domination or destruction of the United States, Israel, the Jewish people, and indeed Western civilization.

One of *The Washington Post*'s foreign correspondents, Karl Vick, set the tone with a highly favorable profile of Ahmadinejad at the beginning of February 2006.[25] He began by putting the president front and center on the world stage:

> On the afternoon of Jan. 4, Iranian President Mahmoud Ahmadinejad reached for the phone and got Latin America on the line. In quick succession, he chatted with President Fidel Castro of Cuba, rang up President Hugo Chavez of Venezuela and, sensing yet another kindred spirit, reached out to Evo Morales, the young firebrand who had just been elected president of Bolivia.

The three Latinos are united in their hatred of the United States, and are distinctly antidemocratic. But Vick did not mention either fact. Instead he called them "relatively poor, disempowered nonaligned nations" who "glory in defying the West." Which was not at all true; all of them, including Iran, have long courted Europe, old and new alike. Their venom was reserved primarily for us. Vick portrayed this as a revival of the so-called Non-Aligned Movement, which despite its title was a useful tool of Soviet foreign policy during the Cold War.

As for Ahmadinejad, he was an inspirational figure, a radical and charismatic leader: "His speeches are great, fantastic, kind of '60s Third World stuff," a Tehran-based European diplomat says.

Vick blamed the United States for any rhetorical excesses

coming out of Tehran. After all, he said, Ahmadinejad's predecessor, Mohammad Khatami, tried to establish a "dialogue of civilizations aimed at rapprochement with Europe and even Washington," but it failed, Vick wrote, "especially after President Bush lumped Iran with North Korea and Iraq in an 'axis of evil' "—which, in Vick's eyes, "strengthened hard-liners who argued that the country must define itself in opposition to the United States." Vick did not point out that Khatami had presided over a wave of censorship and a spate of murders, especially of students and intellectuals who dared to criticize the regime. Nor did he mention that Iran is the world's leading sponsor of terrorism, the driving force behind Hezbollah, Hamas, and Islamic Jihad, which is what bought its ticket into the axis of evil.

The favorable profile continued, "Elected . . . on a populist platform that promised poor Iranians a share of the country's oil wealth," Ahmadinejad "often speaks expansively of the human appetite for 'spirituality' and 'justice,' and refers to himself as 'just a teacher.' " Yet this "teacher" had only recently ordered a systematic crackdown on independent newspapers and blogs, and a bloody crackdown on the working class, as evidenced in the smashing of the bus drivers' union in Tehran in recent weeks. True, Ahmadinejad had promised goodies to the people during his election campaign, but so did every other candidate, and there was no sign that the new president had any intention of delivering on his promise. The bus drivers were asking for decent wages, not for revolution, and they were beaten, arrested, and tortured.

A month later, Vick (writing with David Finkel) attempted to prove that any American attempt to help the Iranian people remove the mullahs from power was doomed to failure. The headline on the front page read: U.S. PUSH FOR DEMOCRACY COULD BACKFIRE INSIDE IRAN, and the lead dumped ice water over hopes for democratic revolution:

> Prominent activists inside Iran say President Bush's plan to spend tens of millions of dollars to promote democracy here is the kind of help they don't need, warning that mere announcement of the U.S. program endangers human rights advocates by tainting them as American agents.

Some Iranian dissidents—hardly household names and certainly not the promised "prominent activists"—attended workshops in Dubai the previous year, and were subsequently arrested when they returned to Iran. The *Post* seems not to have inquired about the treatment inside the regime's prisons, but Vick and Finkel got a catchy quotation from one Emad Baghi: "We are under pressure here both from hard-liners in the judiciary and that stupid George Bush."

Like all citizens of harsh tyrannies, Mr. Baghi was hardly free to speak his mind to American reporters, and in the unlikely event he was unaware of the consequences of criticizing the regime in foreign print, the regime underlined the point by arresting his wife and daughter and subjecting them to interrogation. It would have been very surprising if anyone in Baghi's position had spoken warmly about the American president.

"You know what a vulnerable situation we have here in Iran," Baghi continued. "It was not a good thing to invite us to such a workshop."

Yet Baghi and others still went to it, because they would be able to learn the lessons of the many successful nonviolent democratic revolutions that have swept the world since 1975. They knew it was risky—Baghi was incarcerated for three years in the 1990s, after all—but they were willing to take that risk. Even strong men can be broken, especially when their wives and daughters are in the hellholes of Tehran's infamous prisons, and they can be convinced or compelled to renounce their ideals in order to save the lives of their family members. No news here. Just ask those doomed Soviet citizens who "confessed" at Stalin's show trials.

Vick and Finkel went out of their way to tell the *Post*'s readers that there was no hope of popular insurrection in Iran, and carefully quoted a failed "reformist" saying that nothing good can come from outside help (even though it is hard to find a successful revolution, including our own, that did not have an outside base of support), and that, even if there were hope at one time, that moment has passed. The regime has won: "[T]he capacity for civil society is so depleted that homeowners cannot be bothered to protest the cutting of trees in an eastern Tehran park to make way for a freeway extension."

Vick and Finkel offered this tolerated ecological "violence" to show that resistance to the regime is weakened, when thousands of workers had recently demonstrated against the regime, from Tehran to Khuzestan. Nor did their readers learn about the bravery of Iranian women, who just a week earlier demonstrated in Tehran and were clubbed, slashed, and incarcerated. They knew it would happen, but were willing to sacrifice themselves to show their own courage and the regime's ferocity.

Moreover, the *Post* omitted a crucial element in the story, one that was reported by Eli Lake in *The New York Sun*. A journalist who had attended two workshops in Dubai had spoken with *Post* reporters. He was arrested, and a friend of his "fears that the state is trying to extract a confession through torture." Lake further pointed out that one of the workshops was an entirely private affair, organized by the International Center on Nonviolent Conflict. Not a penny of money from "stupid Bush." But of course, the mullahs don't go in for such distinctions; as always, they lash out at anyone who dares question the legitimacy of their regime. Karl Vick didn't make the distinctions, either.

Then in May, Vick (now sharing the byline with Dafna Linzer) announced[26] nothing less than "a profound change in Iran's political orthodoxy." Many experts may have thought that Iranian clerical fascism was not subject to such dramatic transformation, but Vick believed otherwise. The evidence? The Iranians were calling for direct talks with the United States on the mullahs' project to go nuclear.

Vick and Linzer carefully claimed that this proposal "[erases] a taboo against contact with Washington that has both defined and confined Tehran's public foreign policy for more than a quarter-century."

Notice that little word "public." Because, in fact, the mullahs were chatting with the Great Satan throughout the history of the Islamic Republic, even during the Bush administration. Just ask Richard Haass, the former head of policy planning at the State Department, who organized several such conversations. Or ask George Tenet, who sent some of his spooks to talk to the Iranians. As for earlier periods, you can ask me about the talks with senior ayatollahs in which I was engaged in the mid-1980s. Or call up Robert McFarlane, who went to Tehran to talk to regime officials in 1986. It's an old story, and in all likelihood Vick and Linzer both knew it, so they had to sneak in that "public."

But it isn't even true to say that Iran has not called for, or engaged in, "public" talks with us. There were innumerable talks, quite public ones, about the future of Afghanistan following the decimation of the Taliban regime, and subsequently the Iranian regime eagerly accepted—albeit with all kinds of provisos—the American suggestion that the two countries talk about the future of Iraq.

So there was no change at all, let alone a profound change. The announcement, via the *Post*, was a fairly transparent tactical maneuver, aimed not so much at Washington as at the restive population of Iran. At the time Vick and Linzer were writing, there were demonstrations all over the country, and the regime was working hard to quash them.

- A few days before, following the publication of an offensive cartoon (equating the Azeri people with cockroaches) in the state-run newspaper *Iran Daily*, there were huge demonstrations in Tabriz. According to one eyewitness account there were more than three hundred thousand demonstrators. There were numerous casualties on both sides. The regime bused in thousands of pro-regime demonstrators in an attempt to show popular support for the mullahcracy.
- A month earlier, in reprisal for the killing of twelve regime officials, North Balochistan was bombed by government planes, and hundreds of presumed activists were rounded up, continuing a pattern of systematic repression that has been going on for many years.
- There were big demonstrations on college campuses all over the country, and the regime responded with force. The demonstrations were at least in part in response to new restrictions on political activity at the universities.
- A week earlier, fifty-four Baha'is, engaged in humanitarian activities in Shiraz, were arrested and jailed, hard on the heels of raids on six Baha'i homes, and more than a year of "revolving door" detentions, often with no pretext of legal justification.

All these demonstrations had proximate causes, but all called for an end to the regime and a transition to democracy, as the chants and placards of the demonstrators demonstrated without question. And the demonstrations took place against a background of an ever more aggressive opposition movement. In late April 2006, the Islamist prosecutor in Shadgan was shot by a masked commando. Attacks against government facilities in Ahwaz—in the heart of the oil-producing region—were (and continue to be) ongoing. Two militiamen were assassinated in Shiraz in late April. And we can be sure that many other such actions have been taken, but have gone unreported.

In other words, despite the mounting repression, Iranians of all ethnic backgrounds take advantage of local issues to demand regime change. But this picture was and largely remains lacking from publications like the *Post*, even though it goes a long way to explain the mullahs' disinformation campaign suggesting "profound change." For the mullahs' greatest fear is that they will be overthrown by the Iranian people, and they know that the peoples' greatest hope is that the United States will support them. The mullahs must therefore "prove" to the Iranian people that there is no hope the United States will rally to the cause of Iranian freedom, and the easiest way to do that is to trick the Bush administration into an ongoing dialogue. "You see?" the mullahs will say to the people, "the Americans recognize our legitimacy, they are not calling for our removal, on the contrary they are negotiating with us."

Meanwhile, they have relentlessly waged war against us. Iranian Revolutionary Guards have supplied al Qaeda killers in Iraq with Russian antiaircraft missiles, at the end of a supply route that ran through the bloody hands of Hezbollah. It was all arranged at a meeting in Damascus a month or so before Vick's claim of profound change. Imad Mughniyah, the operational chief of Hezbollah, sneaked into town as part of Ahmadinejad's delegation to oversee the logistics.

Such a regime does not undergo profound change. It just breaks or kills all who challenge it.

The New York Times's man in Tehran, Michael Slackman,

was doing a more serious job, although he, too, had very little to say about the turbulent state of affairs inside the country or the massive repression of the Iranians. He wrote a profile[27] of the Supreme Leader, Ali Khamenei, and found a man who had evolved, who had changed his view of how Iran should be governed as he consolidated his power in the face of various challenges. But the only challenges Slackman discussed were those from political rivals. And while he noted that Khamenei shared Ahmadinejad's hatred of the West (especially America and Israel), Slackman ignored the active support from the regime—which had to be ordered by the Supreme Leader—for terror armies around the world.

Some of our journalists are repeating many of the same errors as their now-despised predecessors who covered the fascist and Nazi regimes and Stalin's Soviet Union, and as others do in reporting from places like China and Cuba. To be sure, it isn't easy to be a correspondent in a tyrannical country. If you report accurately on the regime's nasty practices, you put yourself at risk, either professionally (they might throw you out, which is bad for your career), or personally (you might get beaten, arrested, or even killed). Don't think for a minute that the decapitation of Daniel Pearl was not taken to heart by Western journalists throughout the Middle East. Moreover, journalists in such countries surely know that anyone who talks to them is also running risks, considerably greater than those incurred by the reporters.

When Karl Vick and David Finkel interviewed a man whose family had been arrested (and was no doubt undergoing very unpleasant interrogation in one of Tehran's awful prison cells), they could not possibly have expected him to tell them anything critical of the regime. Had he done so, Baghi's wife and daughter would have paid a terrible price. He knew it, and the *Post*'s journalists knew it too. Yet they went ahead and presented his words as if he were a reliable source, rather than a very frightened Iranian being blackmailed by his government.

One may have sympathy for the plight of the foreign correspondent. When I was living in Italy, one of the biggest stories was, of course, the activities of the Mafia, but very few journalists ever published much about it, for excellent reasons: It was dangerous, and it was always hard to know if your information was any good.

My friend and colleague at *The New Republic*, Claire Sterling, was one of the few who braved it out, at least for a while. In the mid-seventies, she spoke to government officials throughout Europe, traveled to Sicily and found some good sources, and accumulated enough information for a multipart series that she arranged to publish in the *International Herald Tribune*. The first article appeared, and that evening she received a telephone call. It was a voice she had not heard before, a voice with an unmistakable Sicilian accent. "We want to congratulate you," she heard. "That was one of the very best articles about us in recent times." She thanked him. "You're welcome. But surely it would be a mistake to publish any more; it cannot possibly be as good as that article." It was a threat, and she understood it. The next day she informed the editors at the *Herald Tribune* that she didn't want to continue the series.

Claire's behavior was understandable, and no doubt right. It's hard to imagine that any newspaper article is worth your life, after all, and a story about the Mafia certainly is not. But she did not then turn around and publish stories saying that the Mafia did not exist, or that everyone in Sicily was a fan of the *mafiosi*, or that any effort to overthrow the Mafia's regime would inevitably fail. She just stopped writing about them, which is what I think the *Post* should have done with correspondents who in essence served the interests of the Iranian regime. Silence is better than disinformation.

NUKES

The one story that is covered to point of overkill is Iran's nuclear program, and the West's efforts to prevent the mullahs from obtaining an atomic bomb, along with the means to deliver it. Every announcement from the International Atomic Energy Agency (IAEA) gets star treatment in the press and on television, as does almost every statement from top Iranian officials. But despite the saturation coverage, we know surprisingly little about the Iranian program, as demonstrated by the about-face by American intelligence experts in less than two and a half years.

In August 2005, the "intelligence community" issued a National Intelligence Estimate claiming that "Iran is about a decade away from manufacturing the key ingredient for a nuclear weapon, roughly doubling the previous estimate of five years."[28] The Estimate stressed that the experts were not even certain that "Iran's ruling clerics have made a decision to build a nuclear arsenal," although, in a classic example of saying two seemingly incompatible things at the same time, the *Post*'s sources said that "it is the judgment of the intelligence community that, left to its own devices, Iran is determined to build nuclear weapons." In any event, the experts did not think Iran could have a bomb in much less than ten years (although, in yet another wiggle, the experts said there was a "highly unlikely" chance the Iranians might develop an atomic bomb by 2009).

Two years later, in December 2007, a new National Intelligence Estimate was issued, claiming that Iran had "halted its nuclear weapons program in 2003 and that the program remains frozen."[29] And the experts permitted themselves the observation that the "freeze" on the Iranian nuclear weapons program had been ordered because of "international pressure." They did not stipulate the "pressure" they had in mind, but some commentators pointed out that 2003 was the date of the American invasion of Iraq and the overthrow of Saddam Hussein.

Despite the "high confidence" in their conclusion that the weapons program had been suspended some five years earlier, the new Estimate said the experts "do not know whether [Iran] currently intends to develop nuclear weapons." And once again, they predicted that even if the program had been recently resumed, Iran could not have a bomb much before the middle of the next decade, the same forecast they had made in the 2005 Estimate.

There was considerable skepticism about the 2007 NIE, which seemed to many to be more of a policy document than an objective intelligence analysis. The Brookings Institution issued a highly critical analysis,[30] saying that the experts had given an excessively narrow and misleading definition of "nuclear weapons program," and even the director of U.S. National Intelligence, Mike McConnell, appeared to backtrack on February 28, 2008, in evidence to the Senate Armed Forces Committee. McConnell said that Iran had probably halted warhead design and weaponization, but pointed out that Iran's continued enrichment of uranium meant that it was continuing with "the most difficult challenge in nuclear production."

In other words, even if the experts were correct in stating that a covert nuclear program had been "frozen" four years earlier, we admitted that we did not know the current state of affairs (had the "frozen" program been revived?), and did not know enough to forecast with confidence when—or some would say if—Iran would have atomic bombs.

The circle closed again in February 2009, when the *Los Angeles Times* reported that "the Obama administration has made it clear that it believes there is no question that Tehran is seeking the bomb."[31] Leon Panetta, about to be confirmed as

CIA director, put it categorically in congressional testimony: "From all the information I have seen, I think there is no question that they are seeking that capability," and President Obama had referred to Iran's "development of a nuclear weapon" in a press conference, and then changed his language to "pursuit" of weapons.

The uncertainty, and thus the constantly changing language, about an enemy's nuclear program was nothing new. CIA was not prescient in predicting when the Soviet Union would have nukes, either. The first Soviet bomb, which we called "Joe-1" and the Kremlin dubbed "First Lightning," was first tested on August 29, 1949. Three years earlier, on October 31, 1946, the first NIE on the subject was published (secretly, of course), stating "It is probable that the capability of the USSR to develop weapons based on atomic energy will be limited to the possible development of an atomic bomb to the stage of production at some time between 1950 and 1953." And in December of the following year, the CIA's Office of Reports and Estimates wrote, "It is doubtful that the Russians can produce a bomb before 1953 and almost certain they cannot produce one before 1951."[32] By July 1949—about a month before the nuclear test—the forecast remained more or less the same: the "earliest possible date" was mid-1950, while mid-1953 was "the most probable date." And the same projections appeared five days before the test.

The experts did better with China, predicting in 1963 that Beijing would produce an atomic bomb the following year, which they did (the first Chinese nuclear test was on October 16, 1964). But they failed badly with India, failing to foresee the nuclear tests of May 1998. Director George Tenet was sufficiently concerned to create a special panel to figure out what had gone wrong. The panel concluded that the experts wrongly believed that the ruling party in India would act as Western politicians do, promising one thing in a political campaign but failing to deliver once in office. The same risk seems to be present in the current group of experts' efforts to get inside the heads of the ruling mullahs in Tehran. Unlike previous countries, who developed nuclear weapons primarily as a deterrent to their enemies, Iran has already told the world that they would be delighted to nuke Israel.

While all estimates are open to doubt—they mostly rely on information from the International Atomic Energy Agency, and IAEA officials frequently remind us that their data are limited, since the Iranians have barred them from visiting any military sites—the Wisconsin Project suggested that Iran could have developed an atomic bomb as early as March 2009, and could have three bombs by the end of the year.

In December 2001, former President Hashemi Rafsanjani made the shocking statement that "the use of one nuclear bomb inside Israel will destroy everything," whereas the damage to the Islamic world of a potential nuclear retaliatory attack could be limited. "It is not irrational to contemplate such an eventuality."[33] And the regime has staged mass demonstrations that tie the nuclear project to the arrival of the Twelfth Imam, with all the apocalyptic accompaniments.

> . . . in April 2006, in a cult-like ceremony, Ahmadinejad unveiled two metal containers in which were to be found Iran's first independently enriched uranium. Choirs thundered "Allahu Akbar" as exotically clad dancers whirled ecstatically around the containers and lifted them heroically toward the sky in the style of Maoist opera.[34]

Thus did the mullahs marry the cult of the Twelfth Imam to enriched uranium, the indispensable component of atomic bombs. This sort of marriage is what sets the Iranians apart from the other tyrannies of our time, just as an atomic Nazi Germany would have constituted a unique threat to Western civilization.

Indeed the risk of a nuclear Third Reich is what drove Einstein to write to FDR in 1939, thereby initiating the chain of events that led to the Manhattan Project. At the same time, he wrote to friendly officials in the Belgian government (the Belgian Congo was the source of the world's largest deposit of uranium, and Einstein urged the Belgians to do everything in their power to prevent the Germans from laying their hands on it). In that letter, Einstein gingerly suggested that the president might explore the possibility of making American nuclear weapons. Although he was a pacifist, Einstein could not bear the thought of Hitler with nukes.

The thought of Khamenei and Ahmadinejad with nukes is equally terrifying, for they are Hitler's heirs. If that is understood, the issue becomes what to do about it.

4

DEFEATING EVIL

A great deal of intelligence can be invested in ignorance when the need for illusion is deep.

—Saul Bellow

How, then, to defeat the jihadis? Most experts think that the key questions are, Who are they? How many of them are there? Are we fighting a relatively small number of fanatics who have managed to hijack their society, or are we dealing with an entire society gone mad? Do we have to defeat a fringe movement of Islamic extremists, or are we engaged in a clash of civilizations, a global conflict between our Judeo-Christian civilization and Islam itself, and thus almost all of its followers? Are we primarily fighting state-sponsored terrorists, or relatively independent groups?

Similar questions occupied some of our finest pundits during the Cold War. Were we fighting a traditional imperial enemy (the Soviet empire), or were we fighting "international Communism," a mass movement of true believers? Was it necessary to combat Communism everywhere? Or could we just focus on the Kremlin?

You have to do both, but if you have to choose, it's much more effective to go after the headquarters of the global movement. The defeat of the principal sponsor sends shock waves through the movement, and discredits the ideology. All three of the totalitarian movements of the twentieth century claimed to be riding the crest of an irresistible wave. Once they'd been defeated, nobody could believe in their claims of invincibility and inevitability.

Revolutionary regimes, of which the Islamic Republic of Iran is decidedly a case in point, have fallen both because their own people turned against them, and because they were defeated on the battlefield. In each case, the revolutionary ideology was discredited. We humiliated the fascist revolution in the Second World War, and fascism was drained of its mass appeal. Communism lost much of its appeal when the Berlin Wall came down, and the peoples of the Soviet empire demanded freedom and independence. Years before the wall was breached, very few people wanted their country to become a new Bulgaria, and Pope John Paul II once wryly forecast that the last communist on earth would be a North American nun.

There are still communists, but after the fall of the Soviet empire, we don't worry about them nearly as much as we used to. The old Communist parties of Western Europe are either gone (as in Italy) or reduced to dwarf size. As a result, the American government has largely dismantled the heroic radio stations (Radio Free Europe and Radio Liberty) that played such a key role in winning the Cold War.

If the fatal blow to Communism was the fall of the Soviet Union, and the lethal blows to National Socialism and fascism were the defeat of Hitler and Mussolini, in like manner the most important thing we can do to defeat the jihadis is to bring down the regime in Tehran. Year after year, the State Department tells us that Iran is the world's leading sponsor of terrorism. We know in great detail that the mullahs support, train, fund, and indoctrinate all the most lethal terrorist groups, whatever their religious coloration.

No single victory will achieve the defeat of evil, which will be with us so long as there is human life on earth. The defeat of Iran will not bring an end to the jihad, any more than the defeat of the Soviet Union put a stop to all radical leftist anti-American regimes. But without Iran, the key linchpins of the terrorist network will be destroyed, and they will be hard-pressed to survive. Groups like Hezbollah, al Qaeda, Islamic Jihad, and Hamas will suddenly find themselves with much less money than before, and they will suddenly be without the kind of intelligence that only a state can generate. They will be deprived of safe havens, training facilities, and the skilled trainers that have prepared them in such places.

If the Iranian terror masters in Iran were brought down, and replaced with Iranians whose major preoccupations were restoring their society to health, establishing good relations with the West, and putting an end to the outrageous torrent of money that has been given to terrorists (all of which fits well with what we know about Iranian public opinion), the world would be a better place.

There are many ideologies and many charismatic leaders who can inspire blind loyalty, often accompanied by equally blind hatred of their enemies, even to the point of self-immolation. The operational model for today's suicide terrorists comes from Japan's kamikazes in the Second World War. That model remained after the defeat of Japan, and it will survive the defeat of Iran and its closest allies, from Syria to Hezbollah, al Qaeda, and Hamas. But the Japanese abandoned their militaristic ideology after we defeated them, and there is good reason to believe the Iranians would do the same. If that happened, the entire terror network would suffer a potentially fatal blow.

It would not be the first time that the fall of a terror master produced a drop in terrorism. The Soviet Union was a major sponsor of international terror, and when it was defeated, terrorism dropped off as well, until the Iranians, Iraqis, and Saudis took up the slack.

There is more. The defeat of the Tehran regime will weaken the jihadis ideologically as well. Like their totalitarian European and Russian predecessors, the Iranian mullahs are messianics. They believe that their messiah, the Twelfth Imam, will soon rejoin the world of the living, and lead the Islamic armies to a glorious victory over the infidels. We can argue with them from now to kingdom come, but we will never talk them out of that belief (remember Swift's admonition: You can't reason a man out of something he wasn't reasoned into in the first place). But we can do something even more effective: We can prove that their belief is false. We can show the world that their prophecy is false. Nothing is more devastating to a messianic movement than defeat, and no defeat is more effective than bringing down the primary source of the movement's strength.

Unfortunately, many of our policy makers and intellectuals insist on viewing the terrorists in isolation from their state sponsors, as if all you need to create a serious terrorist threat is money and madness. Not so; effective terrorists need many things that come primarily from a nation-state, from safe havens and training facilities to intelligence and the sort of documents needed to avoid notice at international checkpoints.

Greg Sheridan, the foreign editor of *The Australian*, warns us that it is wrong to view terrorist groups as independent actors, because we thereby lose sight of the crucial connection to the proterrorist regimes:

> When U.S. Secretary of State Condoleezza Rice was in India this week, all the talk was about "non-state actors" and the

> challenge they throw up to the international system. The assumption was that the Pakistan-based terrorists responsible for the murders of about 175 people in Mumbai, and the injuries to hundreds more, were non-state actors.
>
> Yet it may be that since the 9/11 attacks in New York, the world has completely misconceived the age of terror.
>
> The radical increase in the lethality, range, political consequence and strategic influence of terrorists comes not from their being non-state actors at all. Instead it comes from their being sponsored by states.[1]

It follows that the best way to diminish the lethality, range, political consequence, and the strategic influence of terrorists is to bring down the states that support them. That is precisely what President George W. Bush said when he announced his administration's policy shortly after the 9/11 attacks: We would not distinguish between terrorist organizations and the states that supported them. As we know, that policy was enforced with regard to Taliban-run Afghanistan and Saddam Hussein's regime in Iraq.

But we have had a very different policy toward Iranian-supported terrorists. We have attacked the terrorists when they came after American and Coalition forces in Afghanistan and Iraq, but we have not taken the conflict to Tehran in any meaningful way. Indeed, President Bush and his leading foreign policy spokesmen consistently said that the United States "seeks a change in Iran's behavior," but certainly not a change in the regime. That language comes word for word from the Clinton years.

Instead of working to bring down the regime in Tehran, the Bush administration fell into the same trap as all its predecessors, from that of the hapless Jimmy Carter to the present. Every president during that thirty-year span, whether Democrat or

Republican, liberal or conservative, eventually convinced himself that we could make a deal with the mullahs, and they all pursued this deal as energetically as conditions permitted.

THE TALKING CURE

Future students of international affairs will no doubt marvel at the persistence with which president after president ran after the mullahs, trying desperately to reach some sort of agreement. Even though these efforts always failed, and even though the outcome was sometimes politically devastating (it probably cost Carter his presidency, and gravely weakened Reagan), the next president always thought it would be different for him. It is said that one form of insanity is the compulsion to repeat the same action over and over again, hoping to get a different outcome. If that is true, then the Iranian threat has driven American presidents crazy for thirty years. And the same craziness has infected the overwhelming majority of politicians (most recently Barack Obama), experts, and pundits, almost all of whom periodically call for negotiations with Iran, as if it had not been tried ad infinitum.

The most extensively documented case occurred during the Clinton administration. We ended all kinds of sanctions against Iran, let all kinds of Iranians (including the national wrestling team) into the U.S. for the first time since the 1970s, we had sporting matches with the Iranians, hosted Iranian cultural events, and unfroze Iranian bank accounts. Then President Clinton and Secretary of State Albright publicly apologized to Iran for purported sins of the past. It all came to nothing when Supreme Leader Khamenei reminded everyone that Iran was in a state of war with the U.S., and that we are their enemies. That put an end to negotiations. The same thing has happened every single time we have tried to reach a "grand bargain" with the Iranian regime.

Last fall, Secretary of Defense Robert Gates—a man well known for his prudence as well as thoughtfulness—remarked on the many failed efforts by the United States to reach some sort of modus vivendi with the Iranian regime.

> Every administration since 1979 has reached out to the Iranians in one way or another and all have failed. Some have gotten into deep trouble associated with their failures, but the reality is the Iranian leadership has been consistently unyielding over a very long period of time in response to repeated overtures from the United States about having a different and better kind of relationship.[2]

Leave aside the fact that, before becoming SecDef, Gates was one of many who recommended "engaging" the Iranian regime in talks; things look different from inside the Pentagon, when daily reports document the extent of Iranian evildoing to our troops in Iraq and Afghanistan, and the murderous activities of their proxies, Hamas and Hezbollah. "Consistently unyielding" is a significant understatement. The "reality," as he puts it, is that there is no reason to believe that the Iranians are interested in anything other than our destruction or domination. They are our enemies, as they have proven over the past thirty years.

Which is not to say they won't talk. They love to talk, and they excel at talking, which they view quite differently from the way we look at "engagement" or "negotiations." We seek durable agreements to resolve fundamental problems; the Iranians are quite capable of striking temporary deals with their worst enemies, fully intending to resume hostilities when circumstances are more favorable.

I saw their methods firsthand. For a few months in the summer and early autumn of 1985, I was the only American official in the room during talks with various Iranians, including some very high-ranking ayatollahs, and I was privy to telephone conversations with Iranian officials in the office of President Mir Hussein Moussavi.

The circumstances certainly favored a positive result, much more so than today's situation (even though there are some important similarities). The Iranians were then at war with Saddam Hussein's Iraq, and they were having a rough go of it. Iraq had the upper hand on the battlefield, and was attacking inside Iran. Iran had hardly any night radar, and once the sun set, the Iraqis routinely bombed Iranian targets, including the cities, which saw a nightly exodus of tens of thousands of people swarming to the safer darkness of the countryside. The regime was becoming more unpopular by the day, as citizens attacked government and religious leaders in the streets. There was even open conflict between different factions of the Revolutionary Guards, and there were reports of workers walking off the oil fields.

Under the circumstances, it was not surprising that the mullahs were prepared to deal, even with the satanic forces of Israel and the United States. The Ayatollah Khomeini, the country's unchallenged tyrant, had to wonder if destiny had turned against him. Iran desperately needed help. And the Iranians had cards to play with us, in the form of several American hostages held by Hezbollah. One of these was particularly important, both to President Reagan and to CIA chief William Casey: William Buckley, the station chief in Beirut. While never admitting they controlled Buckley's fate, the Iranians said that if the relationship between the two countries improved, they would be as helpful as possible in obtaining the release of the American hostages. The Americans replied that the relationship was the central issue, but that Iran would have to call a halt to all terrorist attacks against American targets, and moderate its rhetoric ("death to America," then as now, was loudly chanted in the streets). If that happened, and if Iran helped with the hostages, the United States was prepared to sell weapons to the mullahs as a sign of good faith.

Over the course of several months, the United States sold weapons (and later provided military intelligence), terrorist attacks ceased, and Iranian leaders pointedly omitted America from its enemies list on major public occasions. Two hostages dribbled out, but never Buckley, who was brutally tortured to death. Despite numerous meetings, the relationship was certainly not improved. Each side blamed the other, and there was plenty of blame to share, as I made clear in a detailed account.[3] But, for those who think they can reshape the relationship today, a few important lessons can be learned:

- The degree of ignorance, distrust, and treachery at the highest levels of the Iranian regime is so great that the "process" on their side is almost totally opaque. Officials do not tell one another what is going on, they threaten one another if they suspect anyone is trying to make a deal with the Americans, and their inability to understand the workings of the American government is almost limitless. Our Iran experts constantly bemoan American failure to understand Iran, but the Iranians' ignorance of us is often spectacular. They believed that George H. W. Bush, not Ronald Reagan, was the most powerful man in Washington (after all, he'd run the CIA, which runs much of the world). They did not know who Robert McFarlane was, despite his rank as national security adviser. They believed America controlled Saddam Hussein at will.

- They made promises they never intended to keep, such as promising to arrange for the release of all American hostages if only sufficient arms or spare parts were delivered to Iran. Time after time, meetings were organized on the basis of promises that had been communicated to Washington, only to discover that the relevant Iranian officials had not only not made the promises, but had never been informed of them. This problem is structural, it is not just a question of one personality or another, for it was repeated several times, involving different intermediaries and different Iranian officials.
- The only person who really matters in Iran is the Supreme Leader (Khomeini at the time, Khamenei today), but his power is so awesome that underlings are reluctant to go to him unless they feel they are able to deliver a full package, not just steps en route to an agreement. No bargain can be struck that way. It takes time to work out a deal, but we can't have any confidence that any of the pieces have really been approved, whatever our interlocutors may say. At the end of the process, and only then (assuming that the talks themselves have been approved), will we get approval or rejection. For thirty years, it's been rejection.

The Clinton administration had similar experiences, as shown above. The president and Secretary of State Albright were so convinced that a grand bargain was within their grasp, they publicly apologized to the Iranians for past presumed American sins. But Khamenei rudely brushed them aside; he was not interested in better relations with the Great Satan. This came as a great shock to the Americans, who had been negotiating for months, had lifted elements of the embargo, facilitated cultural exchanges, and the like. Ken Pollack summed it up like this:

> In the Clinton Administration in 1999 and 2000, we tried, very hard, to put the grand bargain on the table. And we tried. We made 12 separate gestures to Iran to try to demonstrate to them that we really meant it, and we were really willing to go the full nine yards and put all of these big carrots on the table if the Iranians were willing to give us what we needed. And the Iranians couldn't.[4]

Pollack's choice of words is spot-on: the Iranians couldn't. They couldn't, because hatred of America is the very essence of the Islamic Republic. To cease that enmity, to call off the thirty years' war against us, would be tantamount to changing the nature of the regime itself. Can you imagine Hitler striking a grand bargain with the Jews, or Mao with the bourgeoisie? It's much the same with the mullahs.

The only really promising element in the talks with Iranians in 1985 came from a senior Iranian government official, who told us he and his allies wanted to work for a better relationship with America, and understood this entailed a change in the nature of the regime. It was never pursued, so I have no idea if he was serious (it could well have been a deception). But he was not the Supreme Leader, and he told us he knew he and his friends would have to challenge Khomeini in order to accomplish his objective.

No doubt there are still senior Iranian officials who want better relations with America, but they are not in a position to deliver it. To do that, they would have to change the nature of the regime. That might be worth discussing, but formal talks between the two governments will not involve such people. We will be talking to representatives of the regime, and they have no interest in regime change. To put it mildly.

We had real leverage on the Iranians back in the mid-1980s, when the regime's leaders actively feared for their survival.

Today's mullahs also fear their own people, and some of their internal enemies are killing mullahs and Revolutionary Guardsmen, just as during the Iran-Iraq War. While Iran is not actively at war, it has suffered severe setbacks on several fronts: Iraq (where its proxy al Qaeda was defeated), Gaza (where its proxy Hamas was defeated), and even Lebanon (where its proxy Hezbollah failed to do anything while Israel was drubbing Hamas). Back in the mid-1980s, Iran was willing to stop calling for the destruction of America for a few months, and put a stop to the killing of Americans by Iranian proxies. Today, the Iranians demand that America apologize and "reform." The terms of reference have been inverted. And sadly, the president seems inclined to accept the inversion.

But if all we want to do is talk, they'll certainly talk. Most talks between Iran and the United States have been private, like those apparently involving former Defense Secretary Perry, and those—little discussed in print so far—with former Ambassador William Miller, a longtime advocate of negotiating with the mullahs who was a back channel between the Obama campaign and Tehran prior to the election of 2008. As the Iranians see it, if we're talking, they can continue to pursue their atomic bomb. So talking is good for them. It's very unlikely to be good for us.

But even the Bush foreign policy team eventually came to believe that a deal could be structured. Contrary to the oft-repeated claim that the George W. Bush administration invariably resorted to force at the expense of diplomacy, the Bush team pursued accommodation with Iran as vigorously as any of the others. From January 2001 to the summer of 2008, scores of publicly reported meetings between top Iranian and American officials took place. As in the past, nothing positive was accomplished, but the Americans redoubled their efforts.

- From November 2001 through December 2002, more than sixteen meetings were held in Geneva and Paris (at least one every month except January 2002) between Deputy Assistant Secretary of State for Near Eastern Affairs Ryan Crocker (who was also serving as the interim envoy to Afghanistan) and senior Iranian foreign ministry officials.
- In November–December 2001, Special Afghanistan Envoy James Dobbins negotiated with Deputy Iranian Foreign Minister Javad Zarif in Bonn, leading to the Bonn Agreement on Afghanistan.
- January 21–22, 2002, Dobbins discussed the Karina-A incident with a senior Iranian diplomat at the Tokyo donors conference for Afghanistan.
- On March 30, 2002, Dobbins discussed the future of the Afghan National Army with an Iranian general, in full uniform, who had been the commander of their security assistance efforts for the Northern Alliance throughout the war.
- In January 2003, acting U.S. Ambassador to Iraq (and NSC Senior Director) Zalmay Khalilzad and Deputy Iranian Foreign Minister Javad Zarif (soon to become UN ambassador) assumed control over the negotiations; they met in Paris.
- On March 16, 2003, Khalilzad and Crocker held a second meeting with Zarif in Geneva. (Five days later, on March 21, 2003, Iranian foreign ministry spokesman Hamid Reza Assefi denied that Zarif and Khalilzad had met.)
- In April 2003, Khalilzad and Crocker held their third meeting with Zarif in Geneva.
- On May 3, 2003, Khalilzad and Crocker held a fourth meeting with Zarif in Geneva.
- On May 4, 2003, Tim Guldimann, the Swiss Ambassador to Iran, faxed to the State Department what he called an Iranian "roadmap" for a comprehensive settlement of issues with the

U.S. (called by some a "Grand Bargain"). (Switzerland routinely handles diplomatic correspondence between Iran and the United States.)

- On October 21, 2003, acting on the basis of an understanding with the United States, German Foreign Minister Joschka Fischer, British Foreign Secretary Jack Straw, and French Foreign Minister Dominique de Villepin met with top Iranian officials in Teheran.
- On November 17, 2003, Secretary of State Colin Powell said, "I think that my three colleagues, the EU three, played a very, very helpful role in going to Tehran . . . and coming back with a very, very positive and productive result." (Time would show that the result was nonproductive, however.)
- In December 2003, there were further talks between Iran and the European Union.
- On November 15, 2004, an agreement was signed in Paris by the governments of France, Germany, the United Kingdom, and the Islamic Republic of Iran. Nine days later, on November 24, Secretary of State Colin Powell said "The United States has been supportive of the Europeans' efforts." On December 13, 2004, expanded talks between Iran and EU began, with explicit American support.
- On January 7, 2005, talks between Russia and Iran on the Moscow proposal (on Iran's nuclear program) ended without a result, with the parties promising to resume talks in February.
- In January 2005, Europe and Iran began trade talks.
- On March 11, 2005, Secretary of State Condoleezza Rice said that the United States would "make an effort to actively support the EU three's negotiations with the Iranians," lift a decade-long block on Iran's membership of the World Trade Organization, and end objections to Tehran obtaining parts for commercial planes.

- Nine months later, on January 12, 2006, the EU three called off nuclear talks with Iran and said Tehran should be referred to UN Security Council. But talks with Iran would continue, and the United States would increasingly attempt to get some sort of deal with the Iranians. On May 31, 2006, in a major policy shift, Secretary Rice announced that the U.S. was willing to join the multilateral talks with Iran if Tehran verifiably suspended its nuclear enrichment program. The U.S. also approved a package of carrots and sticks for EU foreign policy official Javier Solana to present to the Iranians.
- On the same day, May 31, U.S. Ambassador to the United Nations John Bolton was instructed to deliver a message to Iran's UN ambassador, saying that Secretary of State Condoleezza Rice was willing to meet with Iranian officials if the government suspended uranium enrichment. Bolton said he called Iran's ambassador, Javad Zarif, to set up a meeting, but Zarif told him he was instructed by Iran not to meet. Bolton's chief of staff donned sunglasses and a trench coat and dropped off a letter at the mission so each side could say they fulfilled their duties.
- On June 5–6, 2006, Javier Solana flew to Tehran to convey to Iran a package of incentives on behalf of the five permanent members of the Security Council. Solana's message again promised rewards if Iran suspended its uranium enrichment, and specific actions that might be taken if Iran did not accept the package.
- A month later, on July 11, 2006, Ali Larijani, Javier Solana, and the foreign ministers of the P5 plus 1 met in Brussels, with no progress.
- Right after the summer holidays, on September 9, 2006, Solana and Larijani resumed their contacts. The following month, Solana announced that four months of intensive talks had brought no agreement on suspension of Iran's sensitive nuclear

activities, and he added that the dialogue could not continue indefinitely. But it did. The following February, on February 9, 2007, Larijani met with IAEA Chief Mohamed El Baradei.

- The following month, on March 8, 2007, David Satterfield, Rice's senior adviser on Iraq, affirmed U.S. interest in discussions with Iran about the situation in Iraq. Two days later, on March 10, U.S. Ambassador to Iraq Zalmay Khalilzad held a meeting with an Iranian team at a conference of Iraq's neighbors in Baghdad.
- On April 5, 2007, Solana and Larijani held talks in Ankara.
- On May 28, 2007, Ambassador to Iraq Ryan Crocker and Iranian Ambassador to Iraq Hassan Kazemi Qomi met in Baghdad.
- On May 31, 2007, Solana met Larijani in Spain, and they met again, this time in Geneva, the following month (June 22).
- On July 24, 2007, Ambassadors Crocker and Kazemi Qomi held a second round of talks in Baghdad. They held a third round on August 6.
- On August 20–21, 2007, there were extensive talks in Tehran between Iran and the UN's nuclear agency.
- On October 7, 2007, the top U.S. military commander in Iraq, General David Petraeus, accused Ambassador Hassan Kazemi Qomi of belonging to the Quds force of the Iranian Revolutionary Guards Corps, which he charged with "lethal involvement and activities" in Iraq, "providing the weapons, the training, the funding and in some cases the direction for operations" against U.S. and Iraqi forces.
- On October 23, 2007, Solana and the new Iranian nuclear negotiator, Saeed Jalili, met in Rome.
- On November 20, 2007, the U.S. and Iran agreed to a fourth round of Crocker/Kazemi Qomi talks.
- On November 30, 2007, Jalili met with Solana in London.
- On January 11–12, 2008, Mohamed ElBaradei, the director

general of the International Atomic Energy Agency, visited Iran and met Iran's Supreme Leader Ayatollah Ali Khamenei and President Mahmoud Ahmadinejad.

- On January 27, 2008, Khalilzad attended multilateral meetings in Davos, Switzerland, with Iranian Foreign Minister Manouchehr Mottaki and Mojtaba Samare Hashemi, a top adviser to President Mahmoud Ahmadinejad. The State Department later said the contacts were "unauthorized."
- On May 7, 2008, Iranian foreign ministry spokesman Mohammad Ali Hosseini said there was no point in having talks with Washington as long as U.S. forces continued attacking Shiite militias in Baghdad, and therefore a fourth round of talks between the United States and Iran over the security situation in Iraq was unlikely to go ahead.
- On June 14, 2008, Solana traveled to Iran with representatives from the EU three (France, Germany, and the UK) and from China and Russia to present Iran a new offer for negotiations.
- Five days later, on July 19, Undersecretary of State for Political Affairs Nicholas Burns accompanied Solana and representatives of the EU three plus one to meet with Iran's chief nuclear negotiator Saeed Jalili in Geneva.[5]

This impressive list encompasses only the *public* negotiations undertaken by, and on behalf of, the Bush administration; you can be quite certain that there have been many secret contacts, some involving CIA officers, others involving former U.S. government officials. To these must be added events such as the Council on Foreign Relations dinner for Ahmadinejad in New York City on September 20, 2006. The event was organized by the council's president, Ambassador Richard Haass, who had been the head of the policy planning staff at the State Department during Colin Powell's tenure as secretary of state. Haass was a longtime advocate of negotiating with the Iranians, and had argued that the Bush administration had a "historic opportunity" for a breakthrough in relations with the mullahs. He had organized some of the early, secret meetings, of which all that is known is that no historic breakthrough took place.

At the council dinner, many of the guests seemed shocked by Ahmadinejad's attitude. Former National Security Adviser Brent Scowcroft (a "realist" who had advocated negotiating with Tehran) declared that the Iranian president was "a master of counterpunch, deception, circumlocution," and Robert Blackwill, another former high official at State and the NSC, said bluntly, "If this man represents the prevailing government opinion in Tehran, we are heading for a massive confrontation with Iran."[6] The council's own account of the dinner conversation omitted these remarks, simply reporting that Ahmadinejad had "sparred" with the American dinner guests.[7]

There was a secret background to the council's affair, for at that time the top officials of the American government fully expected to have formalized an agreement with Iran. In all likelihood, the council dinner was planned as a celebration of the normalization of relations between the two countries.

A large part of this story was broadcast by the BBC in late February 2009, featuring on-camera testimony from Undersecretary of State Nicholas Burns, who managed the Iran dossier for Secretary Condoleezza Rice. Earlier the previous year, 2008, British Foreign Secretary Jack Straw had convinced Secretary Rice that the Iranians were ready to make a deal. He told her that the Iranians would suspend uranium enrichment in exchange for a lifting of Western sanctions, and a process that would "bring Iran back into the family of nations." Rice agreed, and later convinced President Bush to support the initiative. There were then numerous exchanges between American and

Iranian officials, notably Ali Larijani, then in charge of all negotiations regarding the nuclear project (and the Europeans' favorite Iranian; there were apparently excellent "vibes" whenever Larijani dealt with them). As in the Clinton years, the United States agreed to expand "cultural exchanges" as a sign of good will and openness, and spoke, both privately and publicly, about the "carrots" that would be given to Iran if only the nuclear enrichment activities ceased.

By the end of the summer, the Americans believed they had reached agreement with the mullahs, and the stage was set for a public announcement at the United Nations General Assembly meeting in September. Larijani would come to New York and announce a suspension of the enrichment activities, and Rice would be there to announce that America was lifting sanctions on Iran.

As the denouement approached, the Iranians made an unexpected request: Could the United States quickly issue three hundred visas, as Larijani would be traveling with a large retinue? Rice decided that she didn't want to give the Iranians any excuse for backing out of the deal, and, to the consternation of Homeland Security personnel, staff worked overtime to check the Iranian names against our list of intelligence officers and terrorism enablers. In short order, the visas were issued.

The deal was very closely held; it was not presented at interagency meetings chaired by National Security Council staff members (where such things were normally discussed), and high-level Pentagon officials, as well as top officials in the vice president's office, were unaware of it. Shortly before the deadline, Burns and his assistants went to New York for the happy event.

It never happened. Larijani and the three hundred never came to New York. Instead, Ahmadinejad appeared, and delivered a blistering denunciation of the United States, and a visionary invocation of the imminent arrival of the Twelfth Imam. Burns was annoyed, but remained in Manhattan for several days, awaiting Larijani.

The whole thing was rather like the movie *Groundhog Day*, a farcical replay of the failed "grand bargain" of the Clinton years. Ever since, the mullahs have relentlessly insulted the United States, and proclaimed their total lack of interest in negotiations with us.

As recently as December 2008, for example, former Iranian president Ali Hashemi Rafsanjani, a man generally described as a "moderate," gave a speech at the University of Tehran in which he pronounced:

> There is little difference between statements of Obama and George Bush. . . . For the past thirty years, you [the U.S.] have desired dialogue with us and we didn't talk to you. Now you propose conditions?! . . . Have you forgotten that the Irish McFarlane came here and our authorities were not willing to talk to him, and our second- and third-rate authorities talked to them? . . . I don't expect from someone who considers himself of African race and a suppressed black in America to repeat the words of Bush. . . . We don't want to entangle ourselves with the U.S. and get involved in war. We want to use state-of-the-art science and technology used all over the world. We don't want your persuasion, and your sanctions can't derail our effort."[8]

To people who say, "Why don't we sit down and talk with the Iranians?" the best reply is to remind them of the movie *Goldfinger*. There's a wonderful scene in the middle of the movie when Sean Connery, as James Bond, is spread-eagled on a sheet of gold and there's a laser beam cutting through the gold sheet and about to slice him in half. Gert Fröbe as Goldfinger is standing up on a little balcony looking down. Bond looks up and asks, "Do you expect me to talk?" And Goldfinger replies, "No, Mr. Bond, I expect you to die."

That's exactly the Iranian attitude.

SANCTIONS? INVASION?

Negotiations won't produce either a change of Iranian policy or a change in the Iranian regime. We've got to accomplish one or the other, so if negotiations aren't going to work, what will?

For several years, the Europeans have pretended that a combination of tough negotiations and ever more painful sanctions would do the trick, but they have failed. In truth, I doubt the Europeans ever thought they would get a change in Iranian behavior, and I do not think their policy was aimed at Iran. It was almost certainly aimed at us. They feared we (that is, Bush-the-cowboy) would invade Iran, and so they designed a web of diplomacy and sanctions to forestall American military action.

Economic sanctions and embargoes have generally failed to settle basic conflicts. I do not know of a single case in which economic sanctions have forced an enemy to change its policies, let alone change its regime. We had sanctions against the Soviet Union, with no measurable effect (and we tried the opposite—credits for agricultural purchases—with the same result). The long-standing embargo against Cuba has increased the misery of the Cuban people, but Cuba continues to be an outspoken enemy. The embargo against North Korea did not produce any change in policy from Pyongyang. The embargo against Saddam Hussein's Iraq was equally ineffective in changing Iraqi policies.[9]

All these measures, and others like them, were based on the seemingly rational calculation that sufficient pain would compel sensible leaders to modify their actions. But it didn't work.

Those leaders were committed enemies, and our sanctions simply reinforced their convictions. They were less interested in national wealth than in international victory, and they didn't give a damn about their own people. If some of them starved, it was a worthy sacrifice in a sacred cause.

Those who believe in the efficacy of sanctions point to two cases they think succeeded: Chile and South Africa. It may well be that sanctions catalyzed the fall of the two tyrannical regimes, Pinochet in Chile and apartheid in South Africa. But both regimes thought of themselves as part of "our world," and therefore the sanctions had a huge political and psychological impact. The sanctions stigmatized the Chilean and South African leaders, who were willing to change their policies, and even give up power, in order to mitigate the stigma. Sanctions certainly didn't produce widespread misery.

Nonetheless, advocates of sanctions against Iran believe that the mullahs are uniquely vulnerable to economic pressure because of their lopsided dependence upon petroleum and petroleum products. About 80 percent of Iran's hard currency earnings come from crude oil sales, but a lot of that money goes out of the country to buy refined petroleum products such as heating oil and gasoline. Indeed, just under half of the country's needs for such products are supplied by foreign refineries. Hence, it is argued, if the West can organize an embargo on Iranian imports of gasoline and heating oil, the political system will come under enormous pressure.

The facts are certainly incontestable. Even without an organized embargo, Iran is dependent on oil prices for most of its income, much more so than any other major oil producer. Mohsin Khan, who is the International Monetary Fund's regional director for the Middle East, points out that the Iranian oil industry is enormously inefficient. Iran's break-even oil price is about ninety dollars a barrel (compared with Saudi Arabia at forty-nine dollars, and the Emirates at twenty-three). As oil prices headed south in the autumn of 2008, Khan suggested that Iran would have great difficulty if the prices stayed low for a considerable period of time. Although he did not say so, low oil prices mean less money for terrorism, as for everything else. Further, cheap oil also means even more inflation (which already—according to official statistics, which are always in doubt—reached 26 percent in late 2008).[10]

As Orde Kittrie, of Arizona State's Law School and the Foundation for the Defense of Democracies, noted in late 2008, refined oil products are the Achilles' heel of the Islamic Republic:

> In recent months, Iran has, according to the respected trade publication *International Oil Daily* and other sources including the U.S. government, purchased nearly all of this gasoline from just five companies, four of them European: the Swiss firm Vitol; the Swiss/Dutch firm Trafigura; the French firm Total; British Petroleum; and one Indian company, Reliance Industries. If these companies stopped supplying Iran, the Iranians could replace only some of what they needed from other suppliers—and at a significantly higher price. Neither Russia nor China could serve as alternative suppliers. Both are themselves also heavily dependent on imports of the type of gasoline Iran needs.
>
> Were these companies to stop supplying gasoline to Iran, the world-wide price of oil would be unaffected—the companies would simply sell to other buyers. But the impact on Iran would be substantial.
>
> When Tehran attempted to ration gasoline during the summer of 2007, violent protests forced the regime to back down. Cutting off gasoline sales to Iran, or even a significant reduction, could have an even more dramatic effect.[11]

Ilan Berman, an attentive student of Iran, echoed this view, although his emphasis is somewhat different. Kittrie implies that an embargo of gasoline could galvanize an insurrection, while Berman suggests that the oil price crash provided the United States with a rare opportunity. "If it chooses to do so," Berman argued, "Washington is now in a position to leverage Iran's economic disorder to compel a change in Iranian behavior."[12] Berman called for "squeezing the small number of firms that sell gas to Iran," continuing the financial sanctions that the American government has brought against the Islamic Republic, and issue an ultimatum to foreign companies that do business with Iran: you can do business with them or with the United States.

Increasing the degradation of the country and the pauperization of the Iranian people is not likely to change the regime's behavior, any more than it changed the Soviets' or Saddam's. The mullahs are not going to change, and they will use any sanctions to justify the repression of the Iranian people. Paradoxically, the mullahs welcome open American hostility, in part because it confirms their hatred of us, and in part because it makes it easier for them to blame their own domestic failures on the United States. The mullahs' greatest fear is not that we will invade them, or that we or Israel will bomb them. Their greatest fear is that their own people will remove them from power. That explains their feverish repression of the Iranian people, and their never-ending search for some way to stop Iranians from expressing their contempt for the regime.

The mullahs do not see Iranian dissidents as a purely domestic phenomenon; they treat it as part and parcel of the efforts of the Great Satan to bring them down. They accordingly seize on any pretext to ramp up domestic repression.

They did just that in the second half of 2008, even before the drop in oil prices. Throughout the fall, the regime conducted "security and tranquility" drills in every major city. Armed militias, principally from the dreaded Basij (the most fanatic paramilitary organization), surrounded key buildings, deployed throughout the center of town, and practiced rapid movement from one area to another. This prompted an opposition Web site to describe the atmosphere as an "unofficial martial law."[13]

These drills were coordinated by a new set of security institutions, which brought together local organizations into "security coordination councils." In turn, these were brought under the command of a new "government-military joint working group," headed by a very close friend of Ahmadinejad, Saeed Jalili. Jalili would oversee "all the armed forces of the country and other subdivisions that have a responsibility in the fields of foreign policy, domestic security and defense matters."[14]

The creation of the new structure was announced by Revolutionary Guards General Saeed Mojaradi, the deputy of the chief of staff of the armed forces. Mojaradi spelled out some of the specific threats the new "joint working group" would deal with, chief among them "management of the economic sanctions" (read: embargo-busting activities) and fighting "cultural ploys" and "cultural invasion" (read: shut down all signs of political and cultural dissent).

You could not ask for better evidence that the regime sees all its enemies, domestic and foreign, as a single threat. Totalitarian leaders invariably believe their internal critics are part of an international conspiracy against the system. Ask the victims of Stalin's purge trials. It is no accident that, in the fall of 2008, there was a wave of arrests and executions of people branded "Israeli spies."[15] Interestingly, the "spies" were accused of operating against Iranian "nuclear secrets." This accusation inadvertently gave the lie to the regime's claim that the nuclear program was totally peaceful, for if that were the case, there would be no nuclear secrets to hide.

The campaign against the "Israeli spies" continued into 2009.

In mid-February, the deputy prosecutor Hassan Haddad announced that seven Baha'is would be put on trial for "espionage for Israel, desecrating religious sanctities, and propaganda against the Islamic Republic," and the prosecutor general, Qorban-Ali Dorri-Najafabadi, proclaimed that "there is irrefutable evidence that [the Baha'is] . . . have strong links to the Zionist regime."[16]

REVOLUTION

The massive crackdown confirmed the regime's fear of revolt from below, and the restructuring of the security system strongly suggested that the leaders doubted the loyalty and/or efficiency of the previous arrangement. Both fears were thoroughly justified; in the first week of December, despite the repression, rebellion broke out on university campuses throughout the country. They were so serious that the Islamic Republic News Agency (IRNA) described the Tehran University campus as "a war zone."[17] Student protesters carried banners and posters declaring DOWN WITH THE DESPOTS and WE WANT DEMOCRACY. The top leaders were oddly unprepared for the outburst. Khamenei was scheduled to speak at the Tehran University, Ahmadinejad was slated to appear at the Science and Technology University, and other officials planned to appear at some fifty universities. As the demonstrations broke out, the speeches were canceled, further fueling the enthusiasm of the students. A student spokesman put it simply and accurately: "The dictators dare not show their faces."

The authorities decided to take no risks, sending in thousands of troops to cordon off the campuses in Tehran and at least twelve other cities. Over the next couple of days, an unknown number of students were arrested, and others were beaten up.

The December demonstrations were of a piece with a nationwide pattern of antiregime protest, and while the proximate cause varies from case to case (sometimes because workers or teachers have not been paid for many months—in some cases more than a year, sometimes because the regime threatens to impose new sales taxes, sometimes over treatment of women, and so on), they invariably end up as political, with protestors demanding democracy or freedom, and an end to the regime. The mullahs know that they are facing a population that not only hates them, but holds them in contempt. This means that, as the student revolt shows, many Iranians are no longer afraid of the brutality that awaits them in the regime's prisons. Life under the regime is unbearable, and they do what they can to show how much they want change.

Iran today fulfills all the conditions necessary for revolution. The existing system is widely condemned as a failure, the standard of living is dropping, the rulers are accurately viewed as evil and incompetent, and the once-dominant ideology is rejected by most Iranians. The future under the mullahs offers no hope for improvement; indeed, if oil prices continue between thirty-five and forty-five dollars a barrel, the regime will run out of hard currency by the end of 2009 or early the following year.

Iranians are young, and not inclined to be patient any longer, nor are they pious practitioners of the faith. Seventy percent of the population is under thirty, and these young people are not at all devout (voluntary mosque attendance, like participation in "official" political rallies, is risible in the big cities). They have had it with the regime, and they would welcome the chance to bring it down. Their heroes range from clerics like Ayatollah Boroujerdi to labor leaders and student movement spokesmen.

The greatest threat to the mullahs comes from Iranian women, who are currently in the grips of an epidemic of prostitution. The

Tehran police department conducted an investigation of prostitutes (concluded in January 2009), and came up with results so surprising that no Iranian newspaper would publish them. When the findings were later published in *Der Standard* in Austria,[18] they were spiked in Iran.

Among the surprises:

- Tehran's prostitutes were, overwhelmingly, educated women. Nine out of ten had passed the university entrance exam, and 30 percent were actually university students.
- Most of the prostitutes were not driven to it by desperation and misery. Eight out of ten said they chose to do it, and intended to pursue it only for a short time. "They are content . . . and do not consider it a sin according to Islamic law." One major reason they gave was high fees at the universities.
- Prostitution was thus in large part a search for upward mobility, not an escape from poverty. It is "a way of sharing in the oil-based potlatch that made Tehran the world's hottest real estate market during 2006 and 2007."

It is easy to see why the authorities suppressed the report, for it is hard to imagine any data that could prove so conclusively the failure of the Islamic revolution in Iran. And it goes hand in hand with another spectacular indicator of religious failure: The drop in the fertility rate over the past twenty years is the greatest ever recorded, and it affects all Iranian women, whether in urban or rural areas. Between 1980 and 2006, the fertility rate in Iranian cities dropped from 5.6 to 1.8 (replacement is approximately 2.2), while in the countryside it went from 8.4 to a mere 2.1. Nothing like this has been seen anywhere, even in post-Soviet Russia.

Finally, the entire population, not just the women, is afflicted with large-scale drug addiction, again on an epic scale. A full 5 percent of adult (but nonelderly) Iranians are addicted to opiates (compared to 1 percent of Americans).

In short, the Iranian people are thoroughly alienated from the regime, and would like to see it changed. The despair of the Iranian people—clearly demonstrated in the spectacular levels of drug addiction, prostitution, and infertility—suggests the best strategy for the United States to defeat Iran's war against the West.

Iran is tailor-made for the same political strategy that toppled the Soviet empire: support the dissidents, and demand that the regime give freedom to all its citizens, including the women. We brought down the Soviet empire in this manner with the active support of maybe 5 or 10 percent of the people; how could we possibly fail to bring down the regime in Iran—a country where we know from the regime's own polls that upwards of 70 percent of the people want an end to their government?

The regime knows that their doom is most likely to come from the Iranian people, which is why the mullahs lash out so frequently at various sectors of the population, from the students to the bazaaris, from the workers to the bloggers. In late 2008 and early 2009, the regime announced it had discovered widespread subversion, designed to organize a "soft revolution" of the sort that brought down the Soviet empire. Majlis speaker Ali Larijani described it in terms reminiscent of Stalin's announcement of the infamous Doctor's Plot:

> Since long ago, a comprehensive plot has been under discussion for the arrangement of the regional scene. This plan was gradually brought on the international stage and turned into a paradigm.
>
> This plot aimed at a type of solidarity among the U.S.

> and certain western and Arab countries in the region, and had been hatched to harness Iran through international participation.[19]

Larijani said that the Israeli assault on Gaza was part of this plot, which he claimed had ended in defeat for Israel and the United States. Larijani's announcement was of a piece with an article in FARS,[20] the official state news agency, on January 19, quoting an unnamed person identified as "the director general of the counter-intelligence department of the Ministry of Intelligence." This powerful person announced the discovery of a doctors' plot in Iran.

According to his account, two brothers, usually credited with creating and managing the country's AIDS program (which WHO rates as one of the best in the world) were arrested last September. They traveled a lot, especially to the United States, to stay on top of the latest developments. The head of Iranian counterintelligence said that they were working with the Americans to overthrow the regime.

> During [their] trips the Americans tried to influence those people's thinking and to portray America as Iran's only savior so that after returning to Iran they would put pressure on their officials and create a rift between the people and the officials. . . . During that one-month period, [the Americans] also asked the Iranians to provide an analysis of the situation inside Iran for them. In this way, they wished to collect information [intelligence] about Iran. They particularly asked them about certain issues, such as germs [not further described], non-active defence, [and] the condition of the infrastructure, and those individuals provided them with all the information that they had.

Specific charges followed:

> ... inciting social crises, organizing street demonstrations and interfering in ethnic issues. ... In Azerbaijan Province, they managed to trap a few individuals. ... By raising the issue of ethnic prejudices ... they were trying to incite them and were encouraging them to engage in civil disobedience and non-violent activities.

It's not just the doctors. The mullahs are even afraid of Iran's own history. Over the past several years, artifacts and monuments from Iran's pre-Islamic civilization have been demolished, and in early 2009 the bulldozers destroyed the mass grave at Khavaran, which had contained the remains of most of the political prisoners massacred in the dreadful slaughter of 1988–89,[21] the last years of Khomeini's rule (and the presidency of Ali Khamenei, Khomeini's successor as Supreme Leader). Nobody knows how many were killed, but the numbers are considerable, probably in the area of ten thousand. Some were children, others were within a few weeks of release.

Human rights organizations protested the defamation of the grave, to no effect. With the appropriate symbolism that catastrophe sometimes brings, the site was where the bodies of supporters of the shah, and followers of the Baha'i faith, had been buried. Now it is just a plot of land, with a few freshly planted trees.

The massacres of 1988–89 remain a taboo subject in the Ayatollahs' Iran, and it goes without saying that no serious investigation has ever been conducted by the authorities, even during the presidency of the "great reformer," President Khatami. Indeed, one of his closest advisers, Saeed Hajarian, was inevitably a key figure in the bloodletting, having been a top intelligence official in those years.

The country's leading dissident, Ayatollah Hossein Kazemayni Boroujerdi, delivered a stern rebuke from his prison cell, denouncing the regime's total silence on the desecration of the graves: "While a whole nation is drowning in an ocean of misery, prisons are overflowing with innocent prisoners, and the regime is busily building more prisons to house them."

MOUNTING ANXIETY

The Israeli invasion of Gaza in early 2009 threw Iran's various problems into clear focus. After years of refusing to see Iran's aggressive intentions, most sensible observers of things Middle Eastern now recognize that the most important terrorist organizations, from Islamic Jihad to Hezbollah and Hamas, are essentially Iranian proxies. *Le Figaro* carried a story[22] bluntly headlined IRAN BEHIND HAMAS' GRAD MISSILES, and flatly stated that Hamas military commanders had been trained in Iran and Syria to use the deadliest missiles in their inventory. The battle of Gaza was therefore the second between Israel and Iran in two and a half years, the first being the 2006 conflict with Hezbollah.

The mullahs knew they could lose this battle, and defeat would be very dangerous to a regime like Tehran's, which claims divine sanction for its actions, and proclaims the imminent arrival of its messiah and of the triumph of global jihad. If Allah is responsible for victory, what can be said about humiliating defeat? The mullahs were well aware of the stakes, and it was evident in their behavior.

For some time, the regime in Tehran had shown signs of urgency, sometimes verging on panic. The mullahs organized raucous demonstrations in front of numerous embassies, including those of Egypt (with chants of "Death to Mubarak"), Jordan,

Turkey, Great Britain, Germany, and France. These demonstrations were not mere gestures; the regime's seriousness was underlined on Sunday, January 4, when it offered a million-dollar reward to anyone who killed Mubarak (the Iranians called it a "revolutionary execution"). Significantly, the announcement came at a rally of the Basij, the most radical security force in the country, at which the Revolutionary Guards official Forooz Rejaii spoke. The Egyptians took it seriously; they went on alert of late, looking for the possibility of a Mumbai-type operation in Cairo or elsewhere, and there was a suicide bombing in the capital on February 22.

At the same time, the regime intensified its murderous assault against its own people, most notably hanging nine people on Christmas Eve, and assaulting the headquarters of Nobel Prize Winner Shirin Ebadi.

This intense tempo of activity bespoke alarm in Tehran, which was fully justified by a number of setbacks. First of all, the dramatic drop in oil prices was devastating to the mullahs, who had planned to be able to fund terrorist proxies throughout the Middle East, Europe, and the Americas. Suddenly their bottom line was tinged with red, and this carried over onto their domestic balance sheets, which were already demonstrably shaky (they were forced to cancel proposed new taxes when the merchant class staged nationwide protests). No wonder they seized on any international event to call for petroleum export reductions.

No doubt, the Iranians believed the fall in oil prices was the result of satanic will rather than the shock to demand produced by the runup to $140 per barrel. Not for them the subtleties of the free market; given the way they view the world, they must have been convinced that the same strategy that beggared the Soviet Union—Saudi cooperation with America to hold down prices—was now deployed against them. This belief was no doubt reinforced when the official OPEC cut in petroleum production did not lead to markedly higher prices.

Second, their terror strategy had not been working as well as they wished and expected. Most American and European analysts have not appreciated the effect of the defeat of al Qaeda, Hezbollah, and the Revolutionary Guards Corps in Iraq, but you can be sure that the high and mighty in Arab capitals took full notice. The Iranians not only lost a considerable number of skilled and experienced terror leaders—Imad Mughniyah, the long-time operational chieftain of Hezbollah, was the most important, and Abu Musab al-Zarqawi was close behind, having created al Qaeda in Iraq alongside a network throughout Europe—but also several of their own Revolutionary Guards officers. Some of these were captured, others have defected, and most all have provided details of the Iranian network. This sort of thing is bad for operations, bad for recruiting, and weakened the Iranians' efforts to bully their neighbors into appeasement or more active cooperation.

Third, despite all the efforts to crush any sign of internal rebellion, many Iranians continued to publicly oppose the mullahs. A few weeks before the Israeli strike against Hamas, students at universities all over the country demonstrated in significant numbers, and as one Iranian now living in Europe put it to me, "they were surprised that the regime was unable to stop the protests, even though everyone knew they were planned." This is the background for the new wave of repression, accompanied by an intensification of jamming on the Internet, and an ongoing reshuffle of the instruments of repression; Khamenei and Ahmadinejad have no confidence in the efficacy or blind loyalty of the army or of large segments of the Revolutionary Guards. Most public actions are carried out by the Basij, who are judged more reliable, and repression is less in the hands of the traditional ministries than in the new groups freshly minted in the Supreme Leader's office.

In short, the regime was very concerned about its future, and was not very comfortable with its friends, allies, and proxies. The mullahs know that most Iranians would like to see their leaders treated the same way as the nine executed on Christmas Eve, and like all tyrants, the Iranian despots tried to demonstrate that they dominated both their own country and the region. No surprise, then, that Saeed Jalili, the very important secretary of the "Supreme National Security Council," hit the airwaves of Al-Manar TV to call on "the Arab and Islamic countries and other countries that have an independent will" to fight for a Hamas victory in Gaza and deliver a forceful blow to "the Zionist entity."

But, significantly, when he was asked to get down to brass tacks, Jalili had nothing concrete to say. The Al-Manar interviewer asked him what Iran could do in the Gaza fighting. Jalili's words:

> We believe that the great popular solidarity with the Palestinian people as expressed all over the world should reflect on the will of the Arab and Islamic countries and other countries that have an independent will so that these will move in a concerted, cooperative, and cohesive manner to draft a collective initiative that can achieve two main things as an inevitable first step. These are putting an immediate end to aggression and second breaking the siege and quickly securing humanitarian aid to the people of Gaza.

In other words, the head of the Supreme Council wanted to hold some meetings. It was clear that, when push came to shove, the mullahs could not do anything for their Hamas proxy. The Iranians didn't promise much of anything to the embattled Hamas forces, unless you consider that their "threat" to send boatloads of humanitarian supplies was a serious menace. Indeed, no less a personage than the commander of the Revolutionary Guards, General Mohammad-Ali Ja'fari, blithely said that "Hamas has enough weapons . . . the people in Gaza [do] not need the help of other armies, and [are] capable of dealing with the steps taken by the Zionist regime."[23] In simple English, General Ja'fari told Hamas, "You get 'em, big boy, we're right behind you."

To be sure, there were the occasional calls to Iranians to sacrifice themselves for the cause, but even these lacked all conviction. One Mahdi Kalhar, an adviser to President Ahmadinejad, told a group of students that "Iran must take action . . . we must send [Hamas] aid [in the form of] boatloads of [fighters] on a one-way ticket. . . . An Israeli attack on the boats is nothing to be afraid of—for how else are we to become martyrs?"

No Iranian students gobbled up those one-way tickets; the Iranians never had any intention of sending "fighters" to Gaza. That's not their way. They send others, preferably Arabs, to martyr themselves. Not Iranians.

Many worried that if Israel invaded Gaza, there would be a wave of terrorism against Iran's enemies, and almost surely an assault in northern Israel courtesy of Hezbollah. Aside from a few sparse launchings, it did not happen, and the Hezbollah-dog-that-did-not-bark went hand-in-mailed-glove with the Iranians' sudden preference for conferences rather than suicidal assaults. And as for Iran's Syrian allies, there too the silence was deafening. Syria and Hezbollah may have declared themselves the "winners" of the 2006 battle with Israel, but they didn't seem to be itching for a rematch.

Finally, there was the humiliation of Iraq's Status of Forces Agreement with the United States, against which the Iranians had lobbied for months. Ayatollah Khamenei personally urged Iraqi

Prime Minister Maliki to reject any long-term agreement with the Americans, but Maliki signed it anyway.

In short, the weakness of the Iranian strategy was exposed in early 2001, and no matter how many times the mullahs proclaimed that Hamas had won a signal victory against the satanic forces in Gaza, the actual events no doubt encouraged the tens of millions of Iranians who dream of the day when the regime comes down.

The Iranians do not believe they can do it on their own; they think a successful revolution needs American support, and they are waiting to see some kind of real action by the U.S. to support them against Khamenei, Ahmadinejad, the Basij, and the Revolutionary Guards Corps. They know that if we do not actively support them, they will be slaughtered. What would active support entail? Basically, the same strategy we used to support Soviet dissidents and groups like the Solidarity trade union in Poland.

- Above all, this means open political support from top American officials for the dissidents, and open calls for a change in the nature of the regime. Some American president is going to have to call for an end to Iranian Islamic fascism.
- It means accurate radio and television broadcasting into Iran about events inside Iran itself. This seems counterintuitive, but it is actually easier for Iranians to get information about events in Washington and Los Angeles (they are big Internet surfers; Farsi is the number-four language online) than about what's going on in their own country.
- It means getting revolutionary technology to them, above all, the instruments of contemporary communication: cell phones, satellite phones, phone cards, laptops, servers, and perhaps even BlackBerrys.
- It also means demonstrating the impotence of the regime

> against American power by taking out the terrorist training camps just across the border from Iraq, and the assembly sites for the lethal explosives the Iranians have been providing to Taliban, Mahdi Army, and al Qaeda killers in Iraq and Afghanistan.

THE COUNTERREVOLUTIONARIES

There are many arguments against this strategy: that there is no longer time for a revolution, since Iran will soon have the bomb; that you cannot expect a Muslim country to risk all on behalf of democracy; that there are no leaders inside the country; that the regime's instruments of repression are too powerful. Finally, the skeptics add, anything we do to support the dissidents will only make their lives worse. Repression will increase if we push the mullahs against the proverbial wall, and they will lash out against their opponents.

I am not convinced by the arguments. To take them one by one:

"It's too late." Nobody knows how much time revolutions require before they erupt. There is no science of revolution, and we are usually very surprised when revolutions happen. Given proper support, the Iranians could move very quickly. As for the "deadline," Iran's nukes are hardly a deterrent to revolution. And if anything, if Iran were seen to have nuclear weapons, it would add greater urgency to the need to bring down the regime.

"The Muslims aren't capable of revolution." But Iran had three revolutions in the twentieth century! If there's any country about which it can truly be said that revolutions are "normal," it's Iran.

Furthermore, there's a barely concealed premise of cultural

superiority in the objection, assuming that "they" can't carry out a Western-style democratic revolution. When people say, as they often do, with a glint of ethnic or cultural superiority in their angry eyes, that Arabs or Africans or Persians or Turks just aren't "ready" for democracy, that such people prefer tyrants, or that they have no history of democracy and are hence incapable of it, or they have no middle class, without which no stable democracy can exist, or they believe in Islam, which brooks no democracy, they need to be reminded that some of the worst tyrannies came from highly cultured Christian countries with glorious democratic and humanistic pedigrees, while Iran already had a good constitution in 1906. They also need to remember that Periclean Athens decidedly did not have a large and flourishing middle class, and that the world's biggest Islamic country, Indonesia, is impressively democratic.

Finally, it's silly to claim that a society without long-standing democratic traditions can't create a democracy; if that were true there would never have been any democracies at all, since no society has been democratic forever. All were once governed by despots.

"Lack of leadership." There are certainly dissident leaders. We don't know them all, for the simple reason that they'd be tortured or killed if they were publicly identified. We've seen that happen to student leaders like Batebi or labor leaders like Osanlou or religious leaders like Boroujerdi. But the ongoing demonstrations don't happen all by themselves; each of them has leaders. Indeed, I rather suspect that Iran may have a surfeit, rather than a shortage, of talented leaders.

"The instruments of repression are too powerful." How do you think Iran's security services compare to the KGB? Or the Stasi? Yet revolution succeeded right under their noses.

"Anything done to support the dissidents will only make

things worse." We heard this a lot during the Cold War, and it was proven false. After the fall of Communism, the dissidents told us they had drawn great strength from our support, and that their oppressors had constantly tried to convince them that America wasn't really supporting them at all.

Dissidents know what they're getting into, and for us to refrain from supporting them is to betray them. They are fighting for our common values against an evil that threatens us all. If America stands for anything, it's the struggle against tyranny. This is not just an academic or moral question; tyrants hate America, and will invariably try to kill or dominate us. We need to shed all illusions about the nature of such regimes, above all the nonsense that they are, after all, "just like us," and the false prophecy that whatever differences we have can be resolved by patient negotiation, or cultural exchange, or simple deterrence. We should have learned by now that they are implacable enemies of all free societies, and that the very nature of those tyrannical regimes compels them to attack us as best they can.

We're morally and strategically obliged to support those fighting for freedom within tyrannical societies. It's morally right and strategically sound.[24]

To be sure, revolutions do fail. There are no guarantees. But we live in an age of democratic revolution, and tyrants have been falling with remarkable regularity all over the world for more than thirty years. Revolutions have succeeded in some very unlikely places, from Russia to Ukraine and Georgia, from the Philippines to Lebanon and South Africa. Why not Iran?

Support for revolution is by far the best policy option, and it would be the right thing to do, even if Iran were not the world's leading terrorist sponsor, and were not hell-bent on acquiring an atomic bomb which they say very loudly they intend to use against their satanic enemies.

If we do not bring down the Iranian regime, we will inevitably face the terrible choice so well described by French president Nicolas Sarkozy: bomb Iran, or Iran with the bomb. If we do arrive at that Hobson's choice, it will be a fitting testament to the great failure of the West to deal with this generation's most dangerous and most evil enemies. It will truly be Hell to pay.

CONCLUSION: IRAN AND THE WAR AGAINST THE WEST

Radical Islam inspires mass murder and individual martyrdom for its cause, just as fascism and Communism did in the last century. Osama bin Laden and his ilk rage against the democracies, just as Hitler, Mussolini, and Stalin did. Iranian leaders promise to wipe Israel off the map with nuclear weapons, and to dominate or destroy the Western world, just like their totalitarian predecessors in Russia, Italy, and Germany. Muslim politicians and holy men alike blame the free peoples for the failed societies that define the Middle East. The fanatics who rule in Tehran routinely call the citizens of free countries decadent, corrupt, self-indulgent infidels, worthy of destruction. Just as Hitler, Stalin, and Mussolini planned wars of expansion and gradually built their military power, so the mullahs have become so powerful and so aggressive that Egyptian president Hosni Mubarak told his political followers in mid-December 2008, "The Persians are trying to devour the Arab states."[1] This came less than a week after demonstrations in front of the

Egyptian embassy in Tehran, where the chanting mob added "death to Mubarak" to the usual cries of "death to Israel" and "death to America."

As in the last century, the evil is obvious. Left to their own devices, the mullahs will kill as many of us as they can. As in the last century, we flinch from the necessity of confronting evil until it becomes so powerful it threatens our very survival. Mubarak has neither our power nor our margin of safety; all he can do is warn his friends, and hope they do something about it.

Time will tell, probably quite soon, whether we are going to do something, or wait for our Iranian enemies to strike at us yet again at a time and place of their choosing, as they did in August 2008, against our embassy in Yemen. Evidence of their role in the attack emerged later in the year, in the form of a letter from al Qaeda's number two leader, Ayman al-Zawahiri, to the leaders of the Revolutionary Guards, thanking the Iranians for their invaluable help.[2]

Thus far, having forgotten how close we came to losing the Second World War, we are repeating our past errors. We could lose this war against the Iranian terror masters; our traditional strategic buffer—the oceans—is no longer effective, and our land borders are porous. Moreover, we cannot always identify our enemies by looking at their passports or birth certificates. Some of them are Americans. We should have learned last century that evil people and evil movements can develop inside highly cultured and religious societies, including our own.

That the London killers who attacked London on July 7, 2005, were native Brits surprised a lot of people, which is testimony to our capacity to forget our own history. The 7/7 terrorists were not the first British terrorists (take Richard Reid, the "shoe bomber," for example, or Omar Sheikh, the executioner of Daniel Pearl), nor the first citizens of a Western democracy to embrace the cause of jihad. It is quite easy to compile a long list of native American, British, French, German, Spanish, and Italian terrorists, suicide and otherwise. Mohammed Bouyeri, the assassin of Dutch filmmaker Theo van Gogh, was born and bred in the Netherlands. Our own "Johnny Jihad" (John Walker Lindh), the product of wealthy families in a stylish neighborhood in San Francisco, went to Afghanistan to join the Taliban in the fight against fellow Americans.

These facts were relegated to that part of the spirit that shelters active thought from unpleasant truths. The knowledge that our societies contain people ready to kill us has still not penetrated the awareness of the British people, and, with them, countless Europeans and Americans.

Freedom and democracy do not protect us against such people; indeed, in the past century, free nations elevated them to power, and kept them there until we shattered them on the battlefield. The evil can't be explained by economic misery, or social alienation, or even by the doctrines adopted by the terrorists. The problem lies within us.

Nasra Hassan, who interviewed more than two hundred would-be suicide terrorists and their families, noted in the London *Times* that

> None of the suicide bombers—they ranged in age from 18 to 38—conformed to the typical profile of the suicidal personality. None of them was uneducated, desperately poor, simple-minded, or depressed. Many were middle-class and held paying jobs. Two were the sons of millionaires. They all seemed entirely normal members of their families. They were polite and serious, and in their communities were considered to be model youths. Most were bearded. All were deeply religious.[3]

To be sure, those terrorists Nasra Hassan is talking about came out of Palestinian camps and cities—not from London or San Francisco or Amsterdam—but their profiles are not dramatically different from the terrorists within our own societies. Most of them are not misfits or sociopaths. They are people who find it fulfilling to kill us and destroy our society. This sort of evil cannot be "fixed" by some social program or suitably energetic public affairs strategy, or by "reaching out" to them.

So long as those people remain isolated individuals, awash in modern society, searching for the meaning of life, they will not threaten our society or our way of life. But once they become part of the jihadi movement, they become part of an enemy army. And it's not hard for them to join; most of the mosques in America and Europe are under the sway of radical Islamists, who are funded and instructed by radical imams in Saudi Arabia. Anyone wandering into a mosque anywhere in the Western world is a heavy favorite to hear violent denunciations of the West, and he will have every chance to join the jihad. It should surprise no one to learn that several terrorist cells have been broken up within the United States over the past few years. Not all of these events have made their way into the press, including the breakup of one cell in the District of Columbia, which had an unmistakable Iranian component.

The Iranians excel at identifying potential recruits for terrorist attacks, and then recruiting and training them. A considerable number of the "foreign fighters" that our soldiers encountered in Iraq and Afghanistan were products of Iranian training and indoctrination, and we can be sure that the mullahs have similar people throughout Europe and the United States, waiting for the chance to attack us. From time to time, Iranian "diplomats" at their UN mission in New York City are thrown out of the country after being found photographing subway stations or railroad overpasses.

It is therefore only a matter of time before Iranian-sponsored terrorists strike within the United States, and although the mullahs will do their utmost to cover their tracks, we will eventually have the evidence. That will add to the enormous body of knowledge of their terrorist actions we have built up over the years, most recently on the battlefields of the Middle East. In the course of the Iraq War, we learned a lot about them, both from watching their methods and from interrogating the considerable number of Iranian Quds Force officers we captured. In most cases, they were very cooperative.

While Iran is a terrible threat to us, it is also a very fragile regime. Like all bullies, the mullahs do a lot of threatening and chest-pounding that belies their enormous weakness. Much of what they claim about their own strength is deceptive. Several cases of official announcements of new weapons systems turned out to be hoaxes, including a series of alleged photographs that were Photoshopped.[4]

When we have faced them directly, they have done badly. We defeated their proxy armies in Iraq—a major setback for them—and our Israeli allies delivered another blow by defeating their Hamas proxies in Gaza in early 2009. We have made considerable progress in identifying, blocking, and seizing the regime's money intended for terrorist organizations. If we were serious about bringing down the regime, we would almost certainly succeed.

But we have repeatedly walked away from opportunities to support peaceful regime change in Iran, another bit of eloquent testimony to our amazing ability to blind ourselves to evil, and thereby become an accomplice to it. Many thoughtful people have wrestled with this phenomenon, looking for an answer. Laurel Leff tried to understand why *The New York Times* had not devoted more prime space to the Holocaust, and she concluded that the Sulzbergers' reason was the same as Roosevelt's:

They didn't think they could do anything about it, and so "it was probably easier for bystanders to continue to disbelieve information or reject its salience than to accept their own powerlessness."[5]

That is surely wrong, for there was a great deal that could have been done, if only such people had been willing to do it. Even if Roosevelt was not willing to divert military resources to destroy the death camps, or the railroad lines and highways that led there, he could have mobilized American public opinion in radio addresses, public speeches, and rallies, he could have insisted on saving the victims, and he could have put enormous public pressure on other countries to do the same. At the end of the day, he didn't do it because he didn't want to do it, not because he was powerless.

The same holds for the *Times* and its publisher, Arthur Sulzberger. Had the *Times* conducted an energetic campaign to save the European Jews, it would have had a considerable effect, for many other editors and publishers were inclined to follow the *Times*'s lead, as would many top officials in the American government. A widespread public campaign would have increased the odds of Roosevelt taking action. But Sulzberger did not want to act. He was a fierce anti-Zionist, felt very little kinship with European Jews, did not want a dramatic increase in Jewish immigration quotas, nor a Jewish exodus from Europe to Palestine. Like Roosevelt, he was not powerless. He chose his course of inaction.

The same pattern was repeated in the late spring and early summer of 2009, when, as I predicted in detail, starting on page 168, a revolutionary insurrection erupted in the streets of every major city in the country. The proximate cause for the insurrection was the blatant falsification of the results of the phony "election." It was obvious to most Iranians that the large turnout on June 12 signified a desire to change the composition of the regime, and perhaps even its structure. When the regime announced that Ahmadinejad had been reelected in a landslide, even moderates took to the streets.

The regime had prepared for precisely this sort of mass insurrection, and unleashed the security forces who had been trained to put it down. The savagery of the repression shocked much of the world, making it impossible for anyone in good faith to deny the evil nature of the Islamic Republic.

As our leaders had done throughout the twentieth century, the American government again refused to act. Just as Franklin Roosevelt and other Western leaders had refused to take action against the extermination of the European Jews, and a succession of American presidents had refused to move to save the victims of evil regimes from Iran to Darfur, an American president—this time Barack Obama—and a variety of European leaders again bemoaned the evil, but became accomplices to it by refusing to act. Indeed, not only did the United States fail to support the Iranian people, it openly embraced their enemies. During the worst of the repression, the State Department announced it would welcome Iranian diplomats to Fourth of July celebrations around the world, and President Obama nominated a new American ambassador to Damascus, Syria, Iran's closest ally in the Middle East. Nothing had changed.

At the Eichmann trial in Jerusalem, the story was told of a German soldier named Anton Schmidt. He was executed because he was caught helping Jewish partisans, and Hannah Arendt commented that

> the lesson of such stories is simple, and within everybody's grasp. . . . under conditions of terror, most people will comply but *some people will not*, just as the lesson of the countries in which the Final Solution was proposed is that "it could happen in most places but *it did not happen*

> *everywhere*. Humanly speaking, no more is required, and no more can reasonably be asked, for this planet to remain a fit place for human habitation.[6]

Arendt knew a lot about evil, but she also knew that human beings and human societies were capable of resisting it, and even defeating it, at least for a time. Which is what we must now do.

NOTES

INTRODUCTION

1. See http://history.sandiego.edu/gen/WW2Timeline/camps.html.
2. Augusto Segre, *Memories of Jewish Life: From Italy to Jerusalem, 1918–1960* (Lincoln, NE, and London: University of Nebraska Press, 2008), 297–98. Originally *Memorie di vita ebraica* (Roma: Bonacci Editore, 1979). Rabbi Segre married my wife, Barbara, and me in Rome, shortly before he moved to Israel.

1. SEE NO EVIL, SPEAK NO EVIL

1. Laurel Leff, *Buried by The Times: The Holocaust and America's Most Important Newspaper* (New York: Cambridge University Press, 2005).
2. Robert Conquest, *Reflections on a Ravaged Century* (New York: W. W. Norton, 2000), p. 12.
3. Walter Laqueur and Richard Breitman, *Breaking the Silence* (New York: Simon & Schuster, 1986), p. 14.
4. Martin Gilbert, *Churchill and the Jews: A Lifelong Friendship* (New York: Henry Holt, 2007), p. 186.

5. Ibid., p. 131.
6. Walter Laqueur, *The Terrible Secret* (Boston: Little, Brown, 1980), p. 228.
7. Martin Gilbert, op. cit., p. 195.
8. Raymond Arthur Davies, *Odyssey Through Hell* (New York, I. B. Fischer, 1946), quoted in Laurel Leff, *Buried by The Times: The Holocaust and America's Most Important Newspaper* (New York: Cambridge University Press, 2005), p. 345.
9. See cnn.com/2008/LIVING/11/11/acevedo.pow/index.html.
10. See dtic.mil/dpmo/sovietunion/gulag_study.htm.
11. The report was issued in 1991: aiipowmia.com/reports/exam1.html.
12. Robert Conquest, op. cit., p. 115.
13. Aleksandr Solzhenitsyn, *The Gulag Archipelago 1918–1956* (New York: HarperCollins, 2002), p. 34. Extensive excerpts about Vlasov are available through Google Books.
14. Nicholas Bethell, *The Last Secret* (New York: Basic Books, 1974).
15. Victor Zaslavsky, *Class Cleansing: The Massacre at Katyn* (New York: Telos Press, 2008), p. 59.
16. House Select Committee on the Katyn Forest Massacre, Final Report, 82nd Congress, 2nd Session, 1952. See also House Report 2505, quoted in Zaslavsky, op. cit., pp. 60–61.
17. Robert Conquest, *The Harvest of Sorrow: Soviet Collectivization and the Terror-Famine* (New York: Oxford University Press, 1987), p. 343.
18. Ibid., p. 309.
19. Ibid., p. 320.
20. In *The New York Times,* August 23, 1933. Quoted in Conquest, *Reflections on a Ravaged Country,* p. 123.
21. David Pryce-Jones in *The New Criterion*, January 2003.
22. John P. Diggins, *Mussolini and Fascism: The View from America* (Princeton: Princeton University Press, 1972), p. 40.
23. Ibid., p. 32.
24. Ibid., p. 31.
25. Cf. Jonah Goldberg, *Liberal Fascism: The Secret History of the American Left, from Mussolini to the Politics of Meaning,*" (New York: Doubleday, 2007), pp. 9 ff. for an extensive collection of

pro-Mussolini statements from American leftists and progressives.

26. Renzo De Felice, *Mussolini Il Duce, I. Gli anni del consenso, 1929–1936* (Torino: Giulio Einaudi editore, 1974), pp. 538–87.
27. Cf. "The Question" by Eugene D. Genovese, responses by Mitchell Cohen, Eric Foner, Alice Kessler-Harris, Robin D. G. Kelley, Christine Stansell, and Sean Wilentz, and a final comment by Genovese, in *Dissent* 41: 3 (Summer 1994).
28. *60 Minutes*, December 20, 1998.
29. Michael Dobbs, *One Minute to Midnight: Kennedy, Khrushchev, and Castro on the Brink of Nuclear War* (New York: Alfred A. Knopf, 2008), p. 123.
30. Ibid., p. 6.
31. Philip Gourevitch, *We Wish to Inform You that Tomorrow We Will Be Killed with Our Families: Stories from Rwanda* (New York: Picador, 2004), p. 17.
32. Gil Courtemanche, *A Sunday at the Pool in Kigali* (New York: Random House, 2004), pp. 235–36.
33. Gourevitch, op. cit., pp. 152–53.
34. Samantha Power, "Bystanders to Genocide" in *The Atlantic*, September 2001. See theatlantic.com/doc/200109/power-genocide.
35. See timesonline.co.uk/tol/news/world/iraq/article2326682.ece.
36. See yale.edu/cgp/.
37. From Jeff Jacoby's column in *The Boston Globe*, April 30, 1998.
38. See Michael Ledeen and William Lewis, *Debacle: The American Failure in Iran* (New York: Alfred A. Knopf, 1981), pp. 106 ff.
39. Quoted in Judith Colp Rubin, *Anti-American Terrorism and the Middle East* (Oxford: Oxford University Press, 2004), p. 33.
40. Quoted in Ledeen and Lewis, op. cit., p. 226.
41. Bob Woodward, *State of Denial: Bush at War, Part III* (New York: Simon & Schuster, 2006), pp. 414–15.

2. NONE SO BLIND AS THEY WHO WILL NOT SEE

1. For a discussion of the debate, see Michael Ezra, "The Eichmann Polemics: Hannah Arendt and Her Critics" in *Demokratiya*, Summer 2007. democratiya.com/review.asp?reviews_id=102

2. Philip Gourevitch, *We Wish to Inform You that Tomorrow We Will Be Killed with Our Families: Stories from Rwanda* (New York: Picador, 2004), p. 7.
3. Victor Zaslavsky, *Class Cleansing: The Massacre at Katyn* (New York: Telos Press, 2008), p. 62.
4. Ernesto Quagliarello, "*Per verità di storia,*" in *Nuova Antologia*, n. 2180 (October–December 1991), pp. 127 ff.
5. William Stevenson, *A Man Called Intrepid* (New York: Harcourt Brace Jovanovich, 1976).
6. See Jennet Conant, *The Irregulars: Roald Dahl and the British Spy Ring in Wartime Washington* (New York: Simon & Schuster, 2008).
7. Yuri Slezkine, *The Jewish Century* (Princeton: Princeton University Press, 2004), pp. 200–01.
8. Tony Judt, "The 'Problem of Evil' in Postwar Europe," *The New York Review of Books* 55:2 (February 14, 2008).
9. Translated from Primo Levi, *Se questo è un uomo* (Torino: Einaudi, 1968), pp. 188–89.
10. Michael A. Ledeen, *Freedom Betrayed: How America Led a Global Democratic Revolution, Won the Cold War, and Walked Away* (Washington, DC: AEI Press, 1996).
11. Natan Sharansky, *The Case For Democracy: The Power of Freedom to Overcome Tyranny and Terror* (New York: PublicAffairs, 2004).
12. See http://blogs.abcnews.com/theblotter/2007/06/document_iran_c.html.
13. See http://news.bbc.co.uk/2/hi/south_asia/6750785.stm.
14. See weeklystandard.com/weblogs/TWSFP/2007/10/more_iranian_support_for_the_t.asp.
15. See cnn.com/2007/WORLD/asiapcf/05/30/iran.taliban/index.html?eref=rss_world, and also upi.com/Top_News/2007/10/04/NATO_Irans_Quds_giving_bombs_to_Taliban/UPI-35261191536720/.
16. See voanews.com/english/archive/2008-04/2008-04-30-voa73.cfm?CFID=39818639&CFTOKEN=18224495.
17. See signonsandiego.com/news/world/20070509-0806-iraq-iran.html.
18. See armytimes.com/news/2007/05/military_petraeus_iran_070523w/.

19. See alertnet.org/thenews/newsdesk/N19348645.htm.
20. See washingtonpost.com/wp-dyn/content/article/2007/04/11/AR2007041102121.html?hpid=topnews.
21. See longwarjournal.org/archives/2008/10/iraqi_forces_detain_1.php. This link leads to several others, further documenting Iranian military operations inside Iraq against Iraqi and Coalition forces.
22. Mark Mazzetti, "Documents Say Iran Aids Militias from Iraq," in *The New York Times*, October 19, 2008.
23. Con Coughlin, "Iran Receives al Qaeda Praise for Role in Terrorist Attacks," in *The Telegraph* (London), November 24, 2008.
24. The most complete account appeared in *Asharq Al-Awsat*, a London-based Arabic-language newspaper funded by the Saudi Royal Family. Excerpts appeared in *The New York Times* and *The Long War Journal* on February 4, 2009, in *The Daily Standard* on February 5, and on the same day in the wire of adnKronos International. See adnkronos.com/AKI/English/Security/?id=3.0.2983488416.
25. See news.bbc.co.uk/2/hi/europe/7901101.stm.
26. For a discussion of a recent movie on stoning, cf. http://pajamasmedia.com/michaelledeen/2008/09/06/the-women-continued/.
27. Mercedes Khagani, "Who Supports the Violation of Women's Rights?" in *Rooz*, February 6, 2007.
28. European Foundation for Democracy, "Iran Monitor: Examining the New Totalitarianism," January 2009.
29. This analysis first appeared in Michael Ledeen, "Save the Women, Save Ourselves," in *National Review Online*, April 4, 2005.
30. Daniel Brett, "Iran's Imperial Project in the Shatt al-Arab," British Ahwazi Friendship Society, 2007. Also in http://pajamasmedia.com/bloq/author/britishahwazifriendshipsociety/.
31. Ramin Mostaghim, "Iranian Bank Note Stirs Chain Reaction," *Los Angeles Times,* March 14, 2007. The headline is a rare pun on Iran's nuclear project.
32. Paul Klebnikov, "Millionaire Mullahs," in *Forbes,* July 21, 2003.
33. Hasan Yousefi Eshkevari, "In Mourning for Iranian Press," in *Rooz*, November 30, 2008.
34. "Regime Announces It Has Blocked 5 Million Websites" in *Iran Times,* December 1, 2008.

35. Cf. Laurent Murawiec, *The Mind of Jihad* (New York: Cambridge University Press, 2008), p. 237. Murawiec has many more examples of jihadi bloodlust.
36. Mark Mazower, *Hitler's Empire: How the Nazis Ruled Europe* (New York: Penguin, 2008), p. 589.
37. Matthias Küntzel, "Jew-Hatred and Jihad: The Nazi Roots of the 9/11 Attack" in *The Weekly Standard* 13:1 (September 17, 2007).
38. Steven Stalinsky, "Dealing in Death," in *National Review Online*, May 24, 2004.
39. Elias Canetti, *Crowds and Power* (New York: Continuum, 1978), pp. 152–53.
40. See americanthinker.com/2009/02/turning_universities_into_grav .html.
41. Jillian Becker, *The PLO: The Rise and Fall of the Palestine Liberation Organization* (New York: St. Martin's Press, 1984), p. 77. Cited in Laurent Murawiec, *The Mind of Jihad* (New York: Cambridge University Press, 2008), p. 21.
42. Ibid., p. 37.
43. Quoted in Canetti, op. cit., p. 153.
44. Künzel, op. cit.
45. U.S. Department of State, "Report on Global Anti-Semitism," released by the Bureau of Democracy, Human Rights, and Labor, January 5, 2005.
46. John P. Diggins, *Mussolini and Fascism: The View from America*, (Princeton: Princeton University Press, 1972), p. 490.

3. TO SEE EVIL

1. The Koran, sura 9: 5.
2. Maxime Rodinson, *Marxism and the Muslim World* (London: Zed Press, 1979), pp. 41–42.
3. Laurent Murawiec, *Mind of Jihad* (New York: Cambridge University Press, 2008), p. 137.
4. Bernard Lewis, "Islamic Concepts of Revolution," in P. J. Vatikiotis, ed., *Revolution in the Middle East and Other Case Studies* (Totowa, NJ: Rowman and Littlefield, 1972), pp. 30–40.

5. Cf. Murawiec, op. cit., pp. 256–92.
6. Quoted in Murawiec, op. cit., pp. 262–63.
7. See Melanie Phillips, *Londonistan* (New York: Encounter Books, 2006), pp. 84–85, and also Ed Husain, *The Islamist* (London: Penguin, 2007).
8. There is, of course, a Web site that tracks the latest developments: mahdiwatch.org.
9. Posted on "The Corner," *National Review Online,* November 11, 2008.
10. ISNA, November 16, 2006, translated and quoted by the Iran research section of honestly-concerned.org, November 17, 2006.
11. Mehdi Khalaji, *Apocalyptic Politics: On the Rationality of Iranian Policy* (Washington, DC: Washington Institute for Near East Policy, 2008), p. 24.
12. The Middle East Media Research Institute (MEMRI) Special Dispatch Series - No. 1898, April 16, 2008: "Saudi Cleric Omar Al-Sweilem Extols the Physical Traits of the Black-Eyed Virgins of Paradise." Taken from a video clip posted on the Internet; see memritv.org/clip/en/1741.htm.
13. See http://news.yahoo.com/s/nm/20081204/od_uk_nm/oukoe_uk_iran_clothing.
14. Bernard-Henri Lévy, *Who Killed Daniel Pearl?* (New York: Melville House, 2003). For an excellent summary and discussion, see zeek.net/books_03093.shtml. All quotations are taken from the Web site.
15. Ed Husain, *The Islamist: Why I Joined Radical Islam in Britain, What I Saw Inside, and Why I Left* (London: Penguin, 2007), p. 114.
16. Robert Conquest, *Reflections on a Ravaged Century* (New York: W. W. Norton, 2001), p. 64.
17. The best discussion in English is Franklin Hugh Adler, "Jew as Bourgeois, Jew as Enemy, Jew as Victim of Fascism" in *Modern Judaism*, 28:3, October 2008. Adler has also written at length about this phenomenon in *Telos*, an indispensable source of information.
18. Ibid., p. 15.
19. Cf. Giorgio Amendola, *Intervista sull'antifascismo* (Bari: Laterza, 1976), pp. 10 ff.

20. Quoted in Conquest, op. cit., p. 65.
21. Michael Gove, "Anti-Semitism Is Finding New Allies on Both Right and Left," in *The Times*, April 1, 2008.
22. Rick Santorum, "Hezbollah's Growing Presence in Latin America" in *The Gathering Storm*, August 12, 2008. See eppc.org/publications/pubID.3500/pub_detail.asp.
23. Rick Santorum, "Enemy Roundup" in *The Gathering Storm,* June 19, 2008. See eppc.org/publications/pubID.3434/pub_detail.asp.
24. Cf. Travis Pantin, "Hugo Chávez's Jewish Problem," in *Commentary*, July/August 2008.
25. Cf. Michael Ledeen, "Fisk Vick: Washington Post Hearts Ahmadinejad," in *National Review Online*, February 2, 2006.
26. Michael Ledeen, "Vick Sticks with His Story: The Mullah Spin" in *National Review Online*, May 25, 2006.
27. Michael Slackman, "A Cleric Steeped in Ways of Power," in *The New York Times*, September 9, 2006.
28. Dafna Linzer, "Iran Is Judged 10 Years from Nuclear Bomb: U.S. Intelligence Review Contrasts with Administration Statements," in *The Washington Post*, August 2, 2005.
29. Mark Mazzetti, "U.S. Says Iran Ended Atomic Arms Work," in *The New York Times,* December 3, 2007.
30. See brookings.edu/opinions/2008/01_nie_gordon.aspx?emc=lm&m=212062&l=45&v=859972.
31. Greg Miller, "U.S. Now Sees Iran as Pursuing Nuclear Bomb," in *Los Angeles Times,* February 12, 2009.
32. All these documents are on the CIA's Web site: cia.gov.
33. Quoted in MEMRI, Special Dispatch Series No. 324, January 3, 2002.
34. See matthiaskuentzel.de/contents/iranian-holocaust-denial.

4. DEFEATING EVIL

1. Greg Sheridan, "The Dangerous Illusion of Independent Terrorists," in *The Australian*, December 6, 2008.
2. See defenselink.mil/transcripts/transcript.aspx?transcriptid=4295
3. Michael A. Ledeen, *Perilous Statecraft: An Insider's Account of the Iran-Contra Affair* (New York: Scribner, 1988).

4. See frontpagemag.com/Articles/Read.aspx?GUID=30C6122F-84 E4-49FA-9B44-033193FB9D33.
5. Stephen Rosen, "Bush Administration Contacts with Iran Direct and Indirect, Including More than 28 Seperate Meetings with American Officials of Ambassadorial Rank," in *Middle East Forum*, November 10, 2008. See meforum.org/article/2011.
6. "Iran's Leader Relishes 2nd Chance to Make Waves," *The New York Times,* September 21, 2006, nytimes.com/2006/09/21/world/middleeast/21iran.html.
7. See cfr.org/publication/11498/.
8. Quoted by Michael Rubin in "The Corner," *National Review Online,* December 10, 2008.
9. The two cases of "successful embargoes" are Chile and South Africa. But neither considered itself an enemy of the West, and both wished to be considered members in good standing of the Western world. Consequently, the embargoes had a real political effect, stigmatizing both countries, and encouraging them to alter their (domestic) policies in order to get a sort of Certificate of Good Standing.
10. See http://threatswatch.org/rapidrecon/2008/10/irans-fear-of-low-oil-prices/.
11. See http://online.wsj.com/article/SB122654026060023113.html?mod=djemEditorialPage#printMode.
12. Ilan Berman, "Iran's Economic Dire Straits," in *Forbes,* November 28, 2008.
13. Shervin Omidvar, "Unofficial Martial Law Across the Nation: Police and Security Forces Continue Exercises," in *Rooz*, December 1, 2008.
14. Hossein Bastani, "Change in the Security Structure of Iran?" in *Rooz*, November 30, 2008.
15. Azadeh Mirrazi, "Passdaran Guards' Arrest of a 'Nuclear Spy': Military's Parallel Agencies with the Ministry of Intelligence," in *Rooz*, November 30, 2008.
16. "Iran Prosecutor: Bahais Are Israeli Agents," in *Tehran Times,* February 17, 2009.
17. Amir Taheri, "A Student Rebellion," in *The New York Post,* December 10, 2008.
18. See http://derstandard.at/?url=/?id=1233586592607. Quoted by

"Spengler" in "Sex, Drugs and Islam," in *Asian Times*, February 24, 2009.

19. See http://english.farsnews.com/newstext.php?nn=8711030901.
20. See http://english.farsnews.com/newstext.php?nn=8710301827.
21. Nir Borns and Shayan Arya, "Iran Buries the Past: The Islamic Republic Bulldozes the Mass Graves of Political Victims," in *The Weekly Standard,* February 12, 2009.
22. See ufppc.org/content/view/8254/35/.
23. See honestlyconcerned.info/bin/articles.cgi?ID=KO56309&Category=ko&Subcategory=10.
24. For those who think this idea is no more than a bit of American political rhetoric, note that this doctrine, in these words, was enunciated by French foreign minister Bernard Kouchner.

CONCLUSION

1. See jpost.com/servlet/Satellite?cid=1228728151219&pagename=JPost/JPArticle/ShowFull.
2. Con Coughlin, "Iran Receives Al Qaeda Praise for Role in Terrorist Attacks," in *The Telegraph,* November 25, 2008.
3. See timesonline.co.uk/tol/life_and_style/article543551.ece.
4. See http://pajamasmedia.com/michaelledeen/2008/07/10/sometimes-you- . . . -your-own-goodsometimes-you-can-be-too-tricky-for-your-own-good/.
5. Laurel Leff, *Buried by The Times: The Holocaust and America's Most Important Newspaper* (Cambridge: Cambridge University Press, 2005), p. 348.
6. Hannah Arendt, *Eichmann in Jerusalem: A Report on the Banality of Evil* (New York: Viking, 1963), pp. 230–31.

INDEX